Time to Create

Hands-On Explorations in Process Art for Young Children

by Christie Burnett

Dedication

For Immy and AJ—may you always find time and space to dream

Acknowledgements

My sincerest thanks to my mother, Karen Shaddock, and dear friends Kate Fairlie (http://picklebums.com) and Cath Oehlman (http://squigglemum.com), without whom this book would never have come to life.

My greatest respect and appreciation to the wonderful MaryAnn Kohl, who saw the potential for this book and supported my every step along this new and exciting path.

My thanks to the team at Gryphon House, who took my ideas and made this book what it is today.

To the loyal readers of Childhood101.com—I thank you for giving my words wings to fly around the world.

To the wonderful families and children I worked alongside, thank you for inspiring me to be the best teacher I could be. You taught me so much.

My everlasting love and thanks to my husband, Mathew, for his patience and unquestioning support.

To my daughters, Immy and AJ, for showing me this amazing world afresh, through the eyes of a child.

GH10039
A Gryphon House Book

Time to Create

Hands–On Explorations in Process Art for Young Children

Gryphon House, Inc.
Lewisville, NC

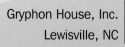

Christie Burnett

Copyright

©2013 Christie Burnett

Published by Gryphon House, Inc.

P. O. Box 10, Lewisville, NC 27023

800.638.0928; 877.638.7576 (fax)

Visit us on the web at www.gryphonhouse.com.

Cover photographs courtesy of Christie Burnett.

Library of Congress Cataloging-in-Publication Data

The Cataloging-in-Publication Data is registered with the Library of Congress for
ISBN 978-0-87659-418-6.

Bulk Purchase

Gryphon House books are available for special premiums and sales promotions as well as for fund-raising use. Special editions or book excerpts also can be created to specifications. For details, contact the Director of Marketing at Gryphon House.

Disclaimer

Table of Contents

Foreword

by MaryAnn F. Kohl

How rich and rewarding the young child's life becomes when art is an important part of the learning process! Art gives every child an opportunity to be individually creative and original, to plan and test ideas, to wonder and explore, and most important, to imagine and to think.

Christie Burnett offers us pages filled with creative art ideas for young children—ideas she has tested, observed, and fine-tuned for success and appeal. What I most appreciate about her work is that she helps us understand the difference between process art and what most people call crafts. It is process art upon which she focuses most strongly. For the purposes of this book, process art is defined as open-ended creativity and exploration of materials; craft is a product-oriented use of materials. Crafts have value within certain contexts, for certainly they ask children to follow directions and complete a project—important skills. But process art encourages children to learn how materials work and behave, to test and try new ideas, and to think! Exploration and learning by doing is a developmentally natural and appropriate way for young children to learn.

I have long been a proponent of process art. In this well-organized, inspiring, and creative book are lots of creative suggestions and ideas that will meet children's needs and encourage them to explore. You can fully expect children will often love their products, too; but, it will be the process that challenges their minds while delighting their sense of aesthetics.

Time to Create: Hands-On Explorations in Process Art for Young Children will bring art to children in ways that foster natural creativity. Children will build communication, self-expression, emotional security, and problem-solving skills. Process art opens a door to the mind where exploration, discovery, and imagination are praised and valued. The end result of all this exploration and imagining is a child who can think and has confidence to look about his world, open to possibilities and wonder.

INTRODUCTION
Children and Art

We want our children to grow into intelligent, socialized adults who make meaningful contributions to their communities. We put a lot of thought, time, and effort into ensuring they develop academically, socially, and even physically, but often put much less emphasis on their creative development. Art experiences provide for a child's development well beyond learning the names of colors or how to draw with a pencil. Well-chosen art experiences offer learning and development opportunities in many areas:

Cognitive skills

- Problem-solving
- Planning
- Trial and error
- Matching attributes
- Patterning
- Sequencing
- Understanding spatial relationships
- Measurement

Physical skills

- Fine motor control
- Eye-hand coordination
- Gross motor control

Language skills

- Communicating both existing knowledge and new ideas
- Symbolic representations of ideas
- Development of vocabulary
- Visual memory

Emotional skills

- Self-expression
- Perseverance
- A sense of self-worth

In order for this development to take place, young children need both time and opportunities to regularly create with a range of art materials. Give your child lots of opportunities to express her unique self and to explore.

In creating with children, the terms *art* and *craft* are often confused. Craft typically involves reproducing an idea or practicing a technique (for example, the initial stages of learning to crochet or knit). Art, however, provides an opportunity for the child to express his individual creativity. Art includes an element of originality as the child's unique response is expressed with open-ended materials. Making art with children is less about the end product (or what it looks like) and more about the process of doing.

I have worked with many parents who are reluctant to offer young children creative materials, as they are concerned about the time these experiences take to prepare and the mess that will result. However, children need very little to be creative or artistic: They will often find joy in a simple paintbrush or crayon and a surface to embellish. Extending their creativity involves expanding the range of materials and surfaces provided, and allowing regular opportunities to express their own ideas and understandings—opportunities to create art.

Children's art is about process above product, about feeling free to create, and about visually sharing their own thoughts and feelings. *Time to Create* will help you to foster children's creativity, allowing you to dip in at a moment's notice and find new ways to engage and involve them in creating wonderfully individual works of art.

Christie Burnett

Reasons Why We Don't Do Art with Children

- I am just not creative or artistic.
- It doesn't look like my child is learning a whole lot.
- It's so messy.
- I don't have the time.
- It takes longer to set up than my child spends creating.
- I don't have the space.
- I don't have the resources.

Reasons Why We Should Do Art with Children

- Art experiences provide important sensory stimulation for young children. A wide range of sensory experiences (touch, sight, sound, smell, and taste) assist babies, toddlers, and preschoolers in developing brain connections essential to later learning. The more regular these experiences, the more these brain connections are developed and reinforced.
- Art provides a vehicle for children to freely and safely express their own ideas and emotions. With thoughtful encouragement, art experiences can be tools for children to communicate what they are learning.
- A child's creative response can tell us a lot about a child and her ideas, thoughts, emotions, and understanding of the world.
- Art experiences in childhood—and, importantly, our attitudes toward them—will influence how a child views her own artistic ability and the level of creative confidence the child has as an adult. What we do now impacts a child's lifelong self-perception as a creative individual.
- Art experiences involve children in communicating symbolically, an important understanding for learning to read and write.
- Being creative requires children to organize their ideas and use a range of thinking skills to manipulate materials and communicate their ideas.
- Many art experiences lay the foundation for a child's ongoing learning of many important language, mathematical, and physical concepts and skills.
- Creating art is fun!

Learning through Art with Infants and Toddlers

Babies and toddlers are continually absorbing information about their world through their senses. Sensory experiences impact directly upon the developing brain and its capacity for lifelong learning. These experiences create new brain connections and strengthen existing ones. The opportunity to explore with age-appropriate artistic materials is the perfect way to engage a young child's senses. As he pushes paint around a page with a stubby brush, feels a chubby crayon in his hand, or bangs upon the tabletop to make handprints, brain development is occurring.

It is important for adults to remember that an infant's or toddler's initial responses to a new creative medium are about exploring the materials. Young children need regular time to explore without the pressure of having to make an end product—and adults must resist the urge to ask, "What is it?" At some stage, toddlers may begin to label their own artwork. This is a first step toward understanding that marks on a page have meaning, which is important to later reading and writing development. Consider the example to the right:

A toddler making circles in the paint with her finger spontaneously says, "Beach."
An adult responds, "What did you see at the beach?"
The toddler replies, "Waves. (pause) Splash."

This simple interaction demonstrates a 21-month-old making an association between experimenting with blue paint and a recent excursion to the beach. The painting experience was not set up to make a painting of the beach; it was simply an opportunity to play with paint and experience the wonder that is glossy, painted color gliding across the page. The association was completely spontaneous and child initiated. She made the mental and verbal connections between the paint and her real-life experience.

Learning through Art with Preschoolers

It is far easier for a child to record his ideas creatively when there are real-life experiences to draw on. A child who has touched, fed, and ridden a horse is much more likely to purposefully use an artistic medium to represent this experience than a child who has only seen a picture of a horse in a book. This is especially relevant to preschool and kindergarten children who are just entering the initial stages of being developmentally able to manipulate familiar art materials to represent their ideas and understandings.

Children enjoy creating when they have new and exciting ideas to express. It is the combination of life experiences and the encouragement to express these ideas through a creative medium that involves children purposefully in artistic endeavors.

How do real experiences help a child to understand and represent his ideas?

You are walking as a family and see a brightly colored rainbow. You talk about the colors you can see and wonder aloud, asking, *How did that rainbow get up into the sky?*

Later, at home, you remind your child about the experience of seeing the rainbow: *Where do we see rainbows? When do we see rainbows? How do you think the rainbow gets up into the sky?*

You listen to your child's theories and ideas and accept them, even if they are different from the scientific facts you know about rainbows. You invite your child to draw (or paint or collage) his idea of how a rainbow gets into the sky. This is different from inviting him to simply draw or paint a rainbow. By observing and talking with your child as he draws, you gain further insight into what he already knows about rainbows. This places you in the best possible position to support him in the process of using a creative material to communicate his own theories and understanding, and to support future learning about the topic. The experience can then be used as a prompt to learn more about the science of rainbows, maybe with a visit to the library for books to guide further research.

This process may feel unusual to your child at first, but repeated opportunities will help him to see that art is a useful way of sharing his ideas.

Accepting Children's Artistic Attempts

"But I can't draw a train. I don't know how."

It is amazing how quickly a child can lose confidence in her own creative abilities. Encourage your child to express her ideas, without judgment from others. There really is no one right way to draw, for example, a tree. Many people will draw a tree to look something like a brown stick with a green cotton ball on top. In reality, trees are all shapes, sizes, and colors. Support your child in her efforts to create in the way that makes sense to her.

To support a child's developing artistic confidence, be encouraging even when it is difficult to see what a child's creation represents. Children need to feel that their ideas will be accepted and respected; mastery comes through repeated attempts. The masters of drawing and painting did not paint an image only once; they revisited an image over and over again, representing it each time in different forms, from different angles, with different materials. Children need this same opportunity to try many different ways of creating and representing an idea without feeling pressured to produce in the one "right" way.

I paint objects as I think them,
not as I see them.
—*Pablo Picasso*

Creating alongside Children

Although it is important for children to see adults using creative tools to represent their own ideas and to see that drawing can be enjoyable and useful, be mindful of how your presence might hamper a child's creative efforts. Depending on the situation and materials at hand, your response to a request to "make with me" might include the following:

- Drawing alongside the child rather than drawing for her. If she needs help to express her own ideas, use questioning as a way of guiding the child's attempts.
- Imitating the types of marks the child is making. If she is exploring with spots, swirls, shapes, or blocks of color, do the same on your own page.
- Using the materials for pattern making rather than representing actual objects.
- Supporting verbally with questioning and encouragement, especially older children engaged in a creative experience that has been specifically designed for them to creatively represent a particular idea.
- Buying time by saying that you are still formulating your idea, thinking about what or how you want to draw. This works to give the child time to continue working on her own masterpiece without adult influence.
- Presenting an object a little differently. Remind yourself that there is never one way to create.

Encouraging Reluctant Artists

How do parents and educators work with a child who is reluctant to create, either because of a complete lack of interest or confidence or a fear of getting it wrong?

Ideas to Help a Child Who Isn't Interested

- Use a child's interests to motivate him to create. For example, a child who is interested in superheroes might like to create a box sculpture of Gotham City. Or, try drawing treasure maps with a child who loves pirates.
- Set a creative challenge. Ask, for example, "Can you use these materials to make a bridge to get from one side of the river to the other?"
- Choose materials and experiences most likely to engage the individual child. A child who doesn't like to draw pictures might like to draw a map or diagram. A child who doesn't like modeling with playdough might prefer to hammer or glue balsa wood pieces into a sculpture.
- Store art materials where they can be seen. You never know when a child might just notice them and ask to make something.
- Make the experience more social by inviting other children to join in, such as during a play date.
- Look for opportunities to take art outside, such as painting on large sheets of paper attached to the fence or drawing with chalk on the pavement.

Ideas to Help a Child Who Lacks Confidence

- Verbally help the child to focus on the task: "Which part of the flower would you like to draw first?"
- Encourage the child by continuing to ask relevant questions or making observations through each step of the process: "What will the pirate ship need to help it sail?"
- Use a photograph or model (for example, an animal figurine) as a visual aid.

Talking to Children about Their Art-Making Experiences

There is one golden rule to observe when talking with a child about her artwork—NEVER assume you know the story behind the creation. Try to avoid asking, "What is it?" or guessing what she has created, as this can be very discouraging if you are wrong (especially for a child who already lacks creative confidence). Instead, try encouraging the child to reflect upon her art making:

- Make a broad observation about what you see: "Wow, look at all those swirls," or "That is very bright pink you have mixed."

- Positively recognize the child's efforts: "The tube was really tricky to attach, but you stuck with it and made it work!"

- Talk to the child about the way she is using the art materials: "That is an interesting way to use the crayon," or, "How did you mix that shade of orange?"

- Ask open-ended questions that encourage thinking and discussion: "How did you do this part?" or, "What were you thinking about when you painted this?"

- Help your child to reflect upon her experience of using the artistic medium: "It's interesting to try using the clay in different ways," or, "What did you enjoy the most about the fingerpaint?"

Wait for answers and do not pressure children to talk, especially when they are engaged in the artistic process of creating. Allow your young child to enjoy a range of creative encounters as part of his growth, development, and learning. Our role as parents and educators is to provide the space, time, and materials for children to create, and to encourage and support them as they respond and share, each in his own unique way.

Choosing the Right Art Activities for Your Child

Before starting an art project or introducing a new art medium, consider whether or not the experience is relevant to the child's interests and level of development. To do this, try asking yourself the following questions:

1. **What is my motivation for choosing this project? Is this project likely to be of real interest to my child?** Sometimes we see an idea and think, "Oh, that is so cute!" or "I would love to try that." Unfortunately, this does not always mean that the idea is within the developmental capabilities of the individual child or even of interest to him.

2. **Is my child likely to find this activity fun and engaging? Is it related to his interests or recent real-life experiences?** Projects that are related to topics or ideas that fascinate a child or to experiences he enjoys provide a positive basis for engagement and are more motivating to the child.

3. **How much of this project can my child do independently?** Children's art should be about the child making art. If you, the adult, are required to undertake 90 percent of the project yourself because it is too difficult for the child to complete, then this may not be the best project to choose. A project that is too difficult can cause frustration and turn a child off from exploring creative activities at all.

4. **Does this project allow my child to respond individually, to express his own ideas? Will the result be unique to my child?** Well-chosen art experiences are those that allow a child to use creative materials to express his own unique ideas in his own way. An art experience that focuses on the end results of five different children's efforts all looking exactly the same provides little room for creativity and individualism and raises a question about whether it can really be labeled art.

Always remember—*unique, individual, creative, experiential,* and *process* are all-important words when it comes to children creating art.

Five Quick and Easy Ways to Mix It Up

Sometimes we get stuck in a rut, offering children the same art materials in the same way, and we wonder why they don't seem as enthusiastic to create anymore. This is the perfect time to mix it up! Changing one little thing can often make a big difference in reinvigorating the creative process for your child.

1. Change the surface.

We don't always need to create on paper. Why not paint on a mirror or a window? Or, collage onto a cardboard box or block of wood? If your child always works on a tabletop, try pinning paper to an easel or taping it to a window.

2. Change the color selection.

Think about ways to change up the color selection—offer soft, pale pastels or shades of one color, or present only warm (or cool) colors.

3. Add texture.

Sand is a wonderful substance and can be easily added to glue, paint, and dough to provide a change in texture. Or, try sawdust, dried lavender, or dried rose petals. Look for other ways to add interest with texture—soft, hard, smooth, rough, wet, or dry.

4. Change the size.

Use a large canvas or roll of paper to create BIG! Or, go small with a tiny piece of fabric or paper.

5. Make it interest based.

Motivate your child by choosing a creative project that fits well with his current interests.

Making Room for Art:
Space to Create

Creating an art space within your home or classroom where children can work regularly on art projects helps them to learn what behavior is expected of them when working in that space and with art materials. Decide whether or not the materials within your art space will be available to your child at all times or only on request. Set and reinforce reasonable boundaries, and make sure your child is clear about your expectations. Depending upon the age of your child, you might choose to keep supplies that require more assistance out of reach, and those they can use independently easily accessible. Having clear expectations and reminding your child regularly of the correct use of the materials and space should help to make the experience less stressful for both child and adult, especially for those who are uncomfortable with the mess that making art can generate.

Art spaces do not need to be large or particularly fancy. Space to work and a place nearby to store art materials will suffice.

- The space can be indoors or undercover outdoors.

- Ideally, the space should have room for a table to work on; a child-sized easel; and a cupboard, shelves, or set of drawers dedicated to storing art materials.
- For many families, an art space needs to work as a multipurpose space, such as the family dining table. Consider the quickest and easiest way to switch from one purpose to the other. In the dining table scenario, one possible solution would be to keep art materials and cleanup supplies ready for use in a dedicated art cupboard within the same room to make setting up and packing away as quick and easy as possible.
- Consider displaying prints or posters of artworks by famous artists within the space for inspiration.

Organizing Art Materials

The quality of art materials available to a child positively impacts the satisfaction found in creative experiences. When investing in good-quality materials, consider how these materials will be stored. Establishing a storage system that is easy to maintain will help your child to assist you in keeping both the art space and materials organized.

- Transparent containers help you to quickly and easily identify what is inside each one.
- Consider storing art materials in individual containers grouped according to type. For example, keep collage materials in transparent storage containers together on one shelf or in one drawer.
- Small baskets, glass jars, and decorative tins or boxes provide useful storage and also look great (which is important if your art space is within a family living space).

- Include a good-sized box or tub for storing useful recyclables.
- Magazine holders are handy for storing recycled magazines and store catalogs, and for books and magazines about art.
- An over-the-door hanging shoe rack with transparent pockets can be a useful investment for storing art materials, allowing you to keep mediums requiring supervision up high and out of reach; those that your child is free to use independently can be placed in the lower pockets.

Displaying Children's Art

One surefire way to show children that you value their artwork, creativity, and learning is to incorporate space for displaying completed pieces within your home or classroom. Incorporating the display space into your child's art space may be one possibility. Alternatively, consider creating a gallery along a hallway or within a shared family space. Once you have chosen a space for your display, there are plenty of hanging options available.

- One of the simplest is to hang string, twine, or ribbon between two hooks, attaching the completed work with miniature clothespins.
- A cork or fabric pin board or a magnetic whiteboard make regularly changing the artwork quick and easy.
- Mounting each piece of artwork on a piece of card stock of the same color takes a little more time but creates a consistent look that can be matched to the décor of the room.
- Displaying artwork in a collection of photo frames may be more time intensive, but it creates a real gallery feel, especially for special pieces. Add small description cards naming the artwork, artist, date, and medium.

Storing Artwork

Children can be prolific artists, creating a mammoth amount of precious artwork over the course of a year, month, or even a day, and decisions often have to be made about which to keep and which to recycle.

It is important to keep those that have special significance. They may have been a "first," such as the first time a child drew a person; they may record an important event or keen interest, or they may even demonstrate a new understanding or mastery of a new skill. Whatever your reason for keeping a piece of artwork, make an effort to date it and note any special significance about the piece.

Once the difficult decision of what to keep has been made, the next step is to find a storage system that works best for you. Consider the following ideas:

- Photograph completed works, print them out, and add them to an album, journaling with the child's name, date, and the story behind the work. Alternatively, photographs can be compiled into a digitally created photo book and printed commercially. Children love to revisit their own creations, and it is very easy to do when they are kept in this form.
- Keep artwork in large storage boxes or tubs (big enough to lay large-sized paper flat). This form of storage will allow you space to store some three-dimensional creations, such as collages or slab clay work, as well.
- Allocate a binder or large art portfolio for each child's art. Larger paper-based artwork can be folded to fit in a plastic sleeve. Photograph three-dimensional works, and add the printed copies to the file.
- Purchase large spiral-bound sketchbooks for your child to draw and paint in. Label each new book with the date your child began using it and the date of completion.
- Scan paper-based artwork, reduce the scans in size, and combine multiple creations into an image collage. Having them commercially printed onto canvas or framing the printed compilation is a wonderful way to preserve and enjoy your child's creativity.
- Share the joy of children's art by using paper-based artwork as wrapping paper, on greeting cards, or as part of a gift.

Supporting Children's Creativity

Time to Create is about seeing the potential of children's art—the unlimited potential for learning, communicating, feeling, and expressing. The ideas within each of the creative medium sections and the included materials lists are intended as a springboard for inspiring your young artist.

As an adult supporting young children's creativity, a few final reminders:

- A child will have a much harder time drawing, painting, or otherwise creating that which he has never seen up close, touched, tasted, heard, or smelled. Rich experiences in the world shared with people they love provide children with a wonderful beginning for creative experiences.
- Listen closely as children wonder aloud about what they see, think, and feel to help you better understand what they know and are learning about the big, wonderful world you inhabit together.
- Accept and respect all of a child's attempts to create as a reflection of her own unique thoughts and ideas at that moment in time.
- Take time to ask good questions—questions that really make a child think.
- Wait to hear a child's answers; don't answer for her or make her rush to respond.
- Provide a place where it is safe to dream, to be curious, and to express ideas freely.
- Provide children with lots of different opportunities to create with different materials, in different ways, and for different purposes.
- Provide an abundance of rich art materials.
- Provide time to create—regular, large, unhurried blocks of time.

Trust and learn from your young child and her interactions with these materials, and remember that above all else, it is the process and the learning that is most important. The final product is just a delightful by-product of these precious early moments of creativity.

Drawing

Yogi and
Booboo Feb 2011

Closely observe a young child drawing, and you will see that drawing is about much more than making scribbles or lines on a page. Children use drawing as a highly symbolic language where marks, shapes, and symbols express their own unique experiences and feelings. Young children's drawings can be their way of representing all sorts of ideas—noises, places, movements, shapes, people, animals, objects, and memories.

For example, when my daughter was just three years old, I took her to see her first children's movie at the theater. She found the experience overwhelming, and we actually had to leave the theater shortly before the movie ended. I have been fascinated by seeing her spontaneously turn to drawing many times since the event as a way of making sense of the experience and the emotions that so obviously engulfed her. Her drawings are always accompanied by lots of talk about what she saw and what it meant. Through representing these ideas, she appears to have found some peace about the whole moviegoing experience. She has moved from her initial reaction of fear, saying that she didn't like the movie, to now proclaiming that she loved it!

Learning

Children's drawings typically progress through a number of developmental stages.

Early drawings are often described as scribbles, a term that should not undermine the importance of this creative stage. Repeated drawing experiences help the very young child to learn that the mark on the page is a response to her own body (finger, hand, arm) actions.

The first tentative marks will change over time, from the backward and forward scribbles of a child's natural hand movement to a greater level of control and making marks in different directions across the page, and then a more circular, scribbling motion will commonly emerge. Given time, a young child will begin to name these marks, and this is the first obvious sign that the child is beginning to realize that ideas and experiences can be communicated visually.

The first purposeful combination of marks that is recognizable to an adult is typically a round shape with dotted facial features and/or straight lines as arms or legs—a first drawing of a human figure. Over time, this combination develops to include more deliberately formed and placed facial features, a circular body, and more detailed features such as hair or fingers.

What may appear random to an adult is actually very detailed—the marks of a toddler.

Add a little more time and fine motor control and a child can more easily combine lines to make squares, triangles, and other shapes, which, when drawn in combination, can represent almost any of the features of her physical world.

During all of these stages, the positive involvement of an interested adult is invaluable. Drawing is much more than just an opportunity to create pretty pictures; it is an essential tool for learning and for communicating.

Doing

Provide children of all ages with many opportunities to draw for different purposes, with a variety of drawing instruments and a range of surfaces.

Drawing from Everyday Experiences

Young children will often draw over and over again images that are important to their everyday lives, such as family members and friends, home, and pets. These are subjects that the child knows well and draws with confidence. It is important that children draw from real experiences in their world, and adults should not expect a child to draw an object if she has had little real-life experience with it.

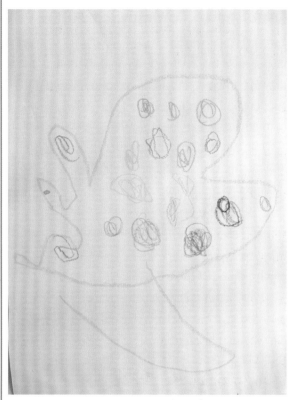

Clockwise from the top left: Four-year-old artist's pet ducks; a three-year-old's Christmas tree; a three-year-old's red car; and two people drawn by a four-year-old.

Drawing to Communicate Learning

If your child has had lots of prior experience drawing, once she is about age three you can support and encourage her to use drawing to communicate learning. Drawing to record learning is by no means limited to pictures but can also incorporate plans, diagrams, brainstorming, instructions, and maps. These can be excellent ways to engage reluctant drawers, especially when the drawing relates to a topic that specifically interests them.

Drawing to communicate learning, four-and-a-half-year-old artist. Titled *Snakes,* and drawn after a lengthy discussion with her mother as to why she always has to wear boots outside at their home in the country.

Here are a few examples of how children can be prompted to use drawing as part of learning:

- Making a terrarium to house snails: Draw all of the items you think we need to collect to put into the terrarium to create a home for the snails.
- Mapping: Now that we are back from our walk, let's draw a map to show the other children which way they need to go to get to the bakery.
- Superheroes: Let's brainstorm the adventures of our superhero before we draw our comic strip.
- Building plans: Can you draw a plan of this construction you have made with the blocks so that we can build it again next time?
- Caring for tadpoles: Let's draw and write some instructions together so that the children in tomorrow's group can see what we have discovered about caring for the tadpoles.

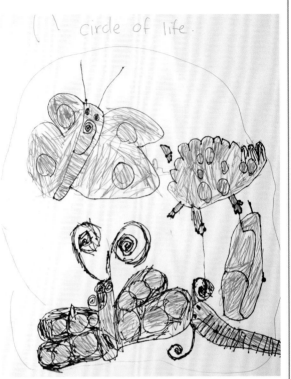

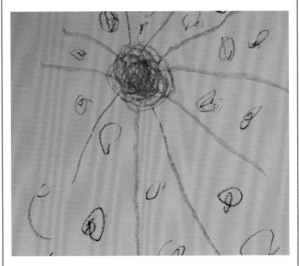

Drawing from Imagination

Although drawing from imagination can begin earlier, once a child reaches the early school years, he is likely to begin drawing more confidently from his own imagination. Take an active interest in the stories that accompany these drawings, to encourage a child to use drawing to represent imaginative ideas creatively.

When a child shares a story describing an image or talks about the process of creating he has undertaken, it only takes a moment to record what the child says about the experience—simply transcribe his words and add the date. Storing your child's reflection with the completed artwork (for example, copying it across to the back of a completed drawing or painting) provides a valuable treasure that you and your child will enjoy looking back on in years to come.

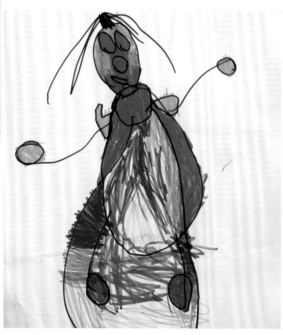

Drawing from Direct Observation

As a child expresses a self-motivated desire for more realism in her images, introducing the idea of drawing from direct observation helps her to see more detail in objects from her world. The child may focus on the colors, shapes, or obvious lines of the object and try to translate these to her drawing. It is this process of seeing and doing that is more important than any finished product.

To introduce your child to drawing from observation, ask her to choose an item of interest. Before your child begins drawing, spend time talking about the object and its features. As she draws, continue to support her efforts by using questioning to focus her attention on the features of the object she draws.

Consider this example of a child and adult looking at and drawing an autumn leaf. The adult asks a series of questions to focus the child's attention:

■ What is the first thing you noticed about your leaf?
■ What shapes can you see? colors? textures? lines?
■ What does this this leaf remind you of?
■ What does your leaf feel like?
■ What do you think these bumpy lines (veins) are?
■ How do you think the color gets into the leaf?
■ What part of the leaf are you going to draw first?

This style of open-ended questioning helps to provide a base of support for the child artist both before and during drawing.

Encouraging Children to Draw

The most effective way to encourage a child to draw is to provide drawing materials regularly, starting when the child is quite young: Chunky, good-quality crayons and sidewalk chalk are the easiest for toddlers to hold and manipulate to make marks. To continue to encourage and engage preschoolers and older children:

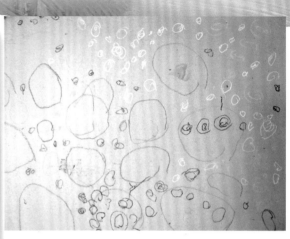

- Periodically introduce new drawing mediums or surfaces to extend the potential for creativity. The Materials and Surfaces List included on pages 124–127 provides a comprehensive list of suggestions.
- Combine drawing media and surfaces in interesting ways, such as working with white or metallic colors on black paper or taping a long length of paper to a wall to create a large drawing area.
- Provide opportunities for drawing on both horizontal and vertical surfaces. Creating on a vertical surface develops fine motor skills, including hand and wrist strength and stability, which are important to the process of learning to write. Examples include drawing with an erasable whiteboard marker on a window or shower curtain or placing a child's favorite drawing medium beside large paper clipped to a freestanding easel.
- Ensure drawing materials are accessible—if not physically, then visually—so that children are prompted to include them as part of their everyday play.
- Encourage the use of drawing as a way to record ideas, discoveries, and everyday experiences.

Seeing

We motivate children to draw and to become
more focused and detailed in their drawing
by asking questions, which helps bring their
attention to details—helping them to think, to
attend to what they are doing, and to remember.

When watching young children draw, notice the
actions they are making, the types of lines and
shapes they are choosing, the words they are
saying, or sounds being made as the drawing is in
progress. These clues all provide insight into what
a child is thinking and expressing.

Talking

Left to make their own choices, young children rarely consider using socially correct colors when drawing. This does not mean that the child does not know what color an object is; rather, his intention in drawing is currently focused elsewhere.

In direct contrast, adults will tend towards the most appropriate color to draw an object or idea they have in mind. An adult asked to draw a leaf will generally choose green or maybe orange. But what about red, yellow, or brown leaves? And which shade of green is correct anyway? The lime green of the leaves of a species of mulberry tree, or the deep, dark green of the leaves on an orange tree? What about the gray-green so prominent in many desert settings? All of these colors (and many, many more) are actually "correct."

We talk often with young children about color, but regularly these interactions are limited to questions such as, "What color is this?" or "What color is the sky?" Phrasing our questions differently can lead to much more interesting and individual responses:

Adult: *What do you think of when you see this color?* (Showing a three-year-old a yellow paint sample card)
Child: *Butter. And lemons. And juice. No, not juice—juice is more orange.*

Or try asking:
What does this color remind you of?
Which colors are happy colors? or sad colors? or mad colors?
Which colors say danger? peace? happiness?
Do you think this is a loud color or a quiet color? Why?

Painting

The bright, glossy, first paint of childhood enchants children with vibrant swashes of color dancing in response to their touch. Unfortunately for most adults, paint equates firstly to unnecessary mess and secondly to declarations of "I'm just not the artistic type!"

In an effort to bridge the gap, this section explores the importance of painting experiences to a child's development alongside simple strategies for managing the mess factor.

Learning

Next, I added a few blobs of red paint to the tabletop. She continued to smooth the paint with her hands, mixing the red into the white, commenting that it was making pink. As we slowly added one new color at a time (white, red, blue, yellow) she slowly, rhythmically, thoughtfully smoothed the colors across the tabletop, mixing each new color with her hands, as if the process were calming, almost meditative.

—Fingerpainting activity with a 22-month-old

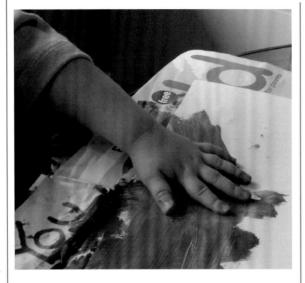

We have discussed the importance of sensory development to young children, and painting is without doubt a valuable multisensory experience. Even at this exploratory age, painting is serious business for the youngest artist, and there is often an element of reverence evident in the child's experimentation. The paint helps the child focus, to center herself and just "be" in one place.

The calming influence of creating is not limited to toddlers or even to paint. Imagine the preschool-aged child who is frustrated or upset by the actions of a sibling. Pounding dough or painting freely on a large paper with a big brush can provide a socially acceptable means of releasing this pent-up emotion. Art materials provide children with a means of expressing strong feelings such as frustration, anger, fear, or sadness, when they do not have the maturity or language to process these emotions in other ways. Simple, open-ended materials such as paint, crayons, clay, or dough serve this purpose best.

Doing

Paintlike Experiences

For babies and younger toddlers who are still likely to put hands to mouth, start simply with edible fingerpaint. Remember that this stage is about engaging all of the senses through the exploration of paint substitutes.

EDIBLE FINGERPAINT

½ cup cornstarch

1½ cups cold water

food coloring

Place ½ cup of cornstarch and 1½ cups of cold water into a small saucepan. Heat over a low heat, stirring constantly until mixture thickens (approximately 2-3 minutes). Allow to cool. Divide into 3-4 portions and add a few drops of liquid food coloring to each.

Other paintlike substitutes for fingerpainting:

- Custard
- Chocolate pudding
- Jelly
- Fruit puree
- Mashed avocado
- Rice pudding
- Whipped cream

Once toddlers are past the stage of mouthing objects, the process of exploring the properties of paint can continue with both fingers and brushes. Toddlers work best with short, stubby brushes.

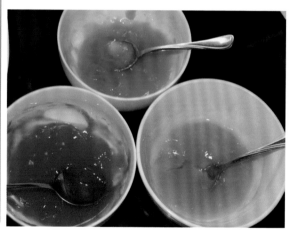

Both child-friendly acrylic paints and diluted food dyes serving as watercolors provide new ways to experiment and a new range of new properties for children to explore.

Provide older toddlers and preschoolers with the opportunity to explore and learn about the properties of paint, still focusing on the change process rather than creating a representative end product.

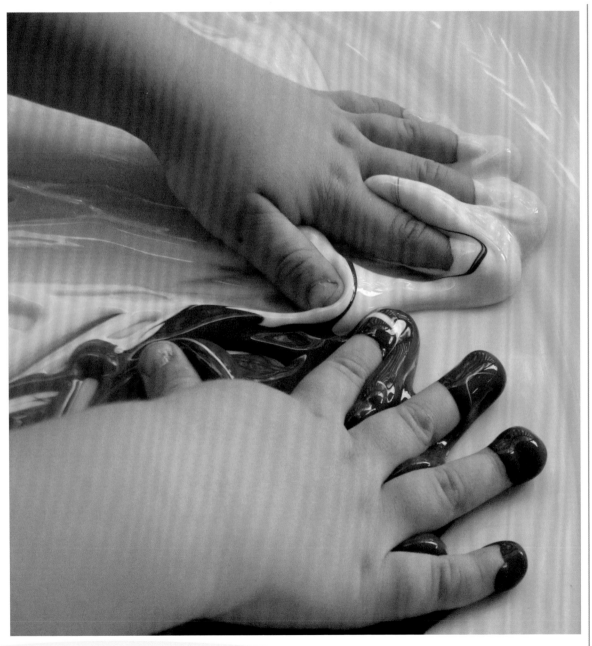

Fingerpainting

Gather your materials:

- Child-friendly acrylic paint
- Glass tabletop, plastic placemat, or cookie tray

Apply paint directly to tabletop, placemat, or cookie tray, and let your child use his fingers and hands to freely explore the rich color and texture of paint. To extend the experience, start with a primary color (red, blue, yellow) and slowly add drops of another to begin experimenting with color mixing. Explore tone by slowly adding drops of one color to a base of white paint to create tints, or add drops of black to a single color to create a succession of darker shades of the original. Experiment with texture by mixing a little sand with the paint. Engage the child's sense of smell by mixing a little lemon or other flavored food essence to the paint.

Shaving Cream Fingerpainting

Shaving cream is thick and smooth to touch, and it smells good, too. But be mindful—a little goes a long way!

Gather your materials:
- Shaving cream
- Food coloring (2–3 colors)
- Cookie tray

1. Apply shaving cream and a few drops of each bottle of food coloring to a cookie tray.
2. Encourage your child to mix away, supervising closely to ensure he does not touch his mouth or eyes.

Shaving Cream Painting

Gather your materials:
- Shaving cream
- Food coloring
- Small paper or plastic cups or a muffin tin
- Paintbrushes
- Glass shower door or window

1. Into each cup, mix a small amount of shaving cream and a few drops of food coloring.
2. Allow your child to paint on a glass shower door or the outside of a window.

Shaving Cream Color Mixing

Gather your materials:
- Shaving cream
- Food coloring or liquid watercolors
- Ziplock bag

1. Squirt a small amount of shaving cream and a few drops of two food coloring into a ziplock bag. Choose two primary colors (red, blue, or yellow) for each bag so the child can experience mixing secondary colors.
2. Squeeze out excess air, seal the top, and let your child squish and pummel to mix the colors. Talk together about the changes you see happening as the colors mix.

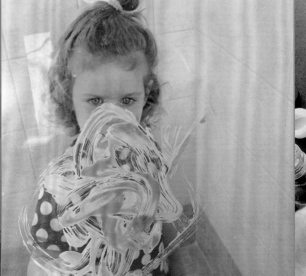

Butterfly Painting

The magic reveal and wonderful symmetry of butterfly painting has made this technique a favorite of toddlers and preschoolers the world over.

Gather your materials:
- Child-friendly acrylic paints
- Paint cups
- Spoons
- Paper painting surface
- Glitter (optional)

1. Fold painting paper in half to form a crease down the center, and then open up flat again.
2. Let your child spoon generous globs of paint all over one half of the paper.
3. Fold the paper in half again, and let your child smooth with her hand to spread the paint inside.
4. Open up to reveal a beautiful butterfly. Sprinkle with glitter if desired.

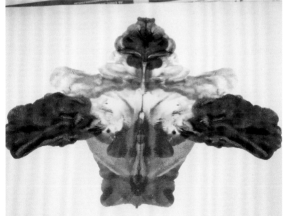

Balloon Painting

Playing with balloons is even more fun when there is paint involved! Safety note: Always supervise your child closely when working with balloons.

Gather your materials:
- Balloons
- Small quantity of sand
- Child-friendly acrylic paints
- Clean Styrofoam trays
- Large paper painting surface

1. Spoon a few tablespoons of sand into the neck of an unfilled balloon. Blow the balloon up to a size that can be held comfortably by your child. Prepare one balloon for each color of paint the child will be using.
2. Add one color of paint to each tray.
3. Let your child dip each balloon into the paint and bounce the balloon all over the paper.

Ball Painting

The process of ball painting is great fun, and the end result is really interesting, especially when you use two or three colors.

Gather your materials:

- Variety of small balls (marbles or golf balls work well)
- Child-friendly acrylic paints
- Paint cups
- Spoons
- Large baking tray, plastic tub, or cardboard box with sides at least 2 inches high
- Paper painting surface

1. Place a sheet of paper into the bottom of the baking tray, tub, or box.
2. Spoon small globs of paint randomly around the paper.
3. Add two to four small balls, and let your child tilt and rock the tray from side to side to spread the paint.

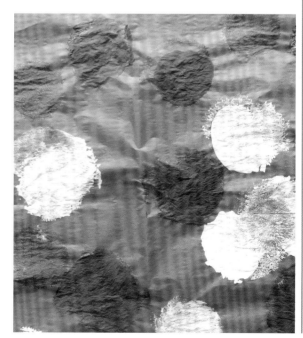

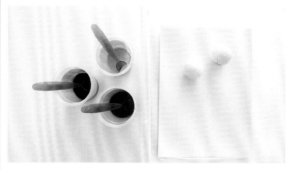

Drip Painting

Young children's art is most definitely about the process of experimenting and exploring, and this experience certainly qualifies as an experiment—and a fascinating one at that!

Gather your materials:

- Child-friendly acrylic paints
- Water
- Paint cups
- Large stretched-canvas painting surface
- Large disposable plastic tablecloth
- Masking tape

1. Place one color of acrylic paint into each paint cup, and thin the paint with a little water so that it pours easily.

2. Choose your painting space carefully. You will need a wall, easel, or something similar to rest the canvas against so that it stands upright. The child should be able to reach the top. Cover the space below with the disposable plastic tablecloth, securing it in place with masking tape. Ensure your drop cloth also

Bubble Painting

This painting experience is great for children who love to blow bubbles. To keep your child from inhaling the paint, poke a small hole about halfway down the straw with a pin.

Gather your materials:

- Food coloring or liquid watercolors
- Shallow bowl
- Dishwashing liquid
- Water
- Drinking straw
- Paper painting surface

1. Combine food coloring or liquid watercolor with a small amount of water and a generous squirt of dishwashing liquid.
2. Give the child a straw, and allow her to blow bubbles until they reach the top of the container.
3. Take a print by gently laying a sheet of paper across the bubbles at the top of the container. Continue blowing or change color and keep taking prints to create a lovely layered effect.

allows for any paint that may overflow off the bottom edge of the canvas.

3. Show the child how to pour the paint from the cup along the top edge of the canvas, watching it run down the smooth surface. Encourage him to pour paint of different colors from the different cups, and discuss which paint drips down the canvas more quickly or more slowly than the others.

Straw Painting

I like to tell children that this is the favorite painting of the Big Bad Wolf! After all, he loves huffing and puffing!

Gather your materials:

- Child-friendly acrylic paints
- Small paper or plastic cups or a muffin tin
- Spoons
- Drinking straw
- Paper painting surface

1. Place one color of paint into each cup, and dilute with an equal amount of water.
2. Encourage your child to spoon generous globs of paint randomly onto the paper.
3. Let him blow through the drinking straw to spread the paint around the page. The harder he blows, the farther it will go!

Fly Swatter Painting

This is the perfect painting experience for active kids, but it is certainly one best enjoyed outdoors!

Gather your materials:

- Clean fly swatter
- Child-friendly acrylic paint
- Plastic lids—one for each paint color
- One large paper, cardboard, or canvas painting surface

1. Squeeze a generous amount of one color onto each plastic lid. Plastic coffee can lids work well.
2. Let your child press a fly swatter onto the paint and then swat onto the painting surface. The imprint of the fly swatter will create interesting patterns.

As preschoolers develop a greater degree of fine motor control, they will enjoy experimenting with different types of paints, painting surfaces, and painting implements. The short, stubby brushes of toddlerhood may prove frustrating for the older child, as they do not allow for the addition of finer details to their creative masterpieces. Provide a range of brushes differing in size, thickness, and style to help your child learn to match the brush to the task.

When choosing art materials, it is generally best to select the highest quality that you can afford. Cheap paintbrushes quickly lose their bristles and must be replaced more often, so it is better to invest in better-quality brushes that will generally last much longer, especially if well cared for. Similarly, paint, crayons, pencils, and other art-making materials will work better and provide a better experience if you can spend a little more to purchase higher quality. For example, cheap, waxy crayons that contain little pigment are at best dissatisfying and at worst just plain frustrating for a child who is working to communicate her thoughts and ideas.

Do not feel limited to the brightly colored acrylic paints commonly used with young children.

Consider also introducing other painting mediums to preschoolers and kindergarteners, such as block and liquid watercolors and watercolor pencils or crayons.

As you introduce any new art-making media, demonstrating simple techniques (such as the process for painting with watercolors shown on page 49) and allowing ample time for open-ended experimentation will help children to achieve more satisfying results.

Let's Talk about Paper

White, black, red, blue, patterned, textured, smooth, thick, thin, translucent, transparent, metallic, matte, tiny, or HUGE—when it comes to paper, you have a great deal of choice available. Fortunately, experimenting with different combinations of paper and art mediums is perfect for all sorts of creative fun! When choosing which paper to use for a creative experience, consider the following.

- **What weight of paper will work best?** Paper is often classified according to its density or the amount of light an individual sheet lets through. A thick cardboard that lets no light through would be labeled heavyweight, while tissue paper falls at the lightweight end of the spectrum.

  When creating with children, matching the weight of the paper to the creative task helps to ensure a greater level of project success. For example, thin, lightweight papers can tear easily, especially if the application is likely to be particularly wet with lots of paint or glue, or heavy due to the choice of collage materials being applied. A medium-weight paper, such as copy paper, is a suitable minimum weight for most painting experiences; however, lighter weight papers such as aluminum foil and cellophane can be mounted onto cardboard before use to make them more durable and less likely to tear.

- **How would a colored, printed, or textured surface work for this experience?** Not all painting or drawing needs to be created on plain white paper. At times, providing different colors, patterns, and textures of paper or card stock will help to encourage variation in the child's creative response.

- **How big shall we go?** Consider also the scale that will work best for your chosen art-making technique. For example, fine delicate work such as using cotton swabs as paintbrushes will generally work best on a smaller painting surface, while fly swatter or balloon painting is perfect for creating on a larger scale. Children have different spontaneous responses with the same art medium when the scale of surface is changed, so regularly changing up the size of the art-making surface is a simple way to encourage children's naturally creative instincts.

Five Suggestions for Interesting Paper Projects

1. Aluminum foil provides a lovely, light-reflecting surface to paint upon with child-friendly acrylics.
2. Tape colored cellophane to a window for drawing upon with markers.
3. On black paper or card stock, offer white, gray, or metallic acrylic paints; crayons; or pastels.
4. Tracing paper provides an interesting translucent surface for drawing on with oil pastels.
5. Try not being square (or rectangular)! Large sheets of paper cut into different shapes and/or with shapes cut out of the middles of them provide interesting variations for painting or drawing.

Create variation by experimenting with different mediums and application methods on a range of surfaces, remembering that variation also comes from providing children with rich, interesting life experiences to represent creatively.

Teaching Children to Use Block Watercolors

Gather your materials:

- Watercolor palette
- Paintbrush
- Small container of water
- Paper towel
- Paper painting surface

1. Wet (or rinse if you are between colors) the brush in the water.
2. Lightly dab the brush on the paper towel to remove excess water. This helps provide the child with a richer, more opaque level of color to paint with.
3. Show the child how to rub the paintbrush on the color she wishes to use to collect the paint onto the brush. The more water on the brush, the more translucent the paint will appear on the paper.
4. Paint! Help the child to repeat this process each time she wants to change colors to avoid creating a dirty brown mixed-up mess!

Teaching Children to Use Watercolor Pencils or Crayons

Gather your materials:

- Watercolor pencils or crayons
- Paintbrush
- Small container of water
- Paper painting surface

For younger children: Show him how to dip the tip of the pencil into the water and then draw with the wet pencil.

For older children: Older children can be shown how to draw with dry watercolor pencils and then enhance areas of the drawing by using a wet paintbrush to carefully paint over the colored-in areas of the image.

Six Easy Ways to Control the Mess

1. Choose your time wisely. A block of time first thing in the morning or immediately following rest time, when everyone is fresh and unrushed, works best.
2. Choose your space wisely. Take everything you will need outside if it is less stressful for you to be messy outdoors. Indoors, choose a space with enough room away from walls and furniture, and use drop cloths or plastic tablecloths where necessary.
3. Choose a project appropriate to the interests and development of your child. If your child is not interested, don't force the activity. If you can, leave the materials set up for him to come back to when he's ready. If this is not possible, do the activity some other time.
4. Make sure everything you need is set up before you begin.
5. Invest in a good-quality, plastic, child-sized apron with long sleeves and elasticized cuffs, which covers clothing but still allow your child to move freely.
6. Make cleanup a priority by having a plan and everything ready—bucket of soapy water, wet facecloth or wet wipes—before paint is even put to paper.

Teaching Children to Help Wash Brushes

Preschoolers and kindergarteners can be taught the following easy process for washing paintbrushes as part of the cleanup process.

1. Put one squirt of liquid hand soap into each child's hand.
2. Turn the water on slowly, just a trickle.
3. Rub the paintbrush gently in the soap in the child's hand.
4. Rinse and rub the brush under the water.

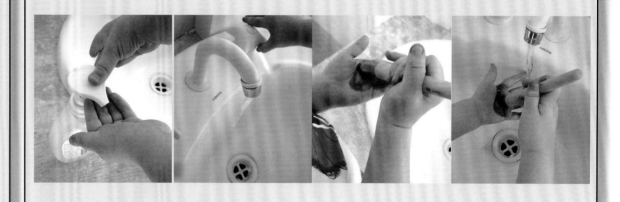

Seeing

Visiting an art gallery is an excellent way to engage a child's interest in art. Looking at and talking about the work of recognized artists provides children with the opportunity to observe a range of art techniques and processes.

Tips for Visiting an
Art Gallery with Children

- Visit on a weekday morning when the gallery will generally be quieter.
- Don't try to see everything in one visit. Wherever possible, research online and plan your visit, choosing those exhibits that will most likely interest your child.
- Older children might also like to look online for notices about permanent and visiting exhibitions and might make a plan for their visit.
- Enquire beforehand about special exhibits or activities for children, especially during school holidays and summer break.
- Once at the gallery, stop and look at what interests your child even if it isn't part of your plan.
- Take regular breaks for snacks and to use restrooms. Wherever possible, provide time outdoors for children to expend excess energy or to just sit and be quiet.
- Use open-ended questioning or make simple observations to encourage your child's thoughts as she looks at artwork.
- Often, galleries have postcards of major artwork available for free or for a small cost. These can be a cheap and easy resource to take home to stimulate further creativity.

Talking

Working with paint provides lots of opportunity for art talk about both the way the paint is manipulated by the artist and the results of the artist's hard work. Encourage your child to reflect on her artistic endeavors with gentle questioning and observation:

- Color: "I noticed you made a secondary color—orange. What colors did you mix to make orange?" or "What happened to the blue when you mixed it with the white?"
- Texture: "I can see that you are painting with very gentle brush strokes," or "How did you make the gray paint look like clouds?" (Caution: Only name a painted work if your child has used the label first.) or "What happened when you were using the thin, watery paint?"
- Thoughts and feelings: "What were you thinking about when you were making this painting?" or "How does your finished painting make you feel?"
- Give gentle reminders: "Take your time; paint slowly," or "Be gentle with the brush," or "We have plenty of paper."

Northern Landscape, 1970. Robert Juniper, oil on canvas.
On display in the Art Gallery of Western Australia, Perth.

Printmaking

"Up. Down. Up. Down."

"One star. Two stars. Three stars. Four stars."

"A red one and then a yellow one and now another red one."

Put simply, printmaking experiences involve creating multiple copies of a mark or image. Printmaking is a wonderful way to extend a child's art experiences beyond drawing and painting, using creative supplies he is already familiar with. It also provides learning far beyond the act of creating. In the process of doing, a child is feeling, observing, describing, and developing an understanding of concepts important to later learning of both literacy and mathematics.

Learning

Printmaking communicates knowledge, ideas, thoughts and feelings in a highly symbolic manner, similar in nature to writing. As a child works to make repeated images with printmaking materials, she is actually physically experiencing the concept that an object reproduces the same impression time and again. The image, icon, or texture demonstrates a sense of permanency. This concept supports the early literacy understanding that letters have consistent formations and that words remain the same each time a book is read.

Printmaking also provides opportunities for learning important mathematical concepts:

- Matching attributes
- Identifying similarities and differences
- Recognizing and creating patterns
- Describing attributes such as color, shape, texture, and number

Finally, printmaking provides the means for young children to symbolically represent their own ideas and understandings. The printmaking experiences suggested here are all suitable for young children and are presented in an approximate order of difficulty to assist you in selecting which will best suit your child.

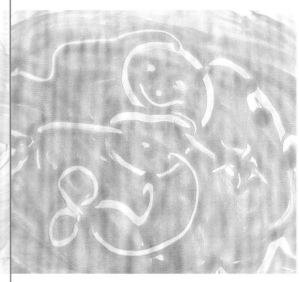

Doing

Monoprinting

Monoprinting is a natural extension of fingerpainting and continues the process of engaging the child with the sensory input that is important to early brain development.

Gather your materials:

- A smooth surface to work upon—a glass tabletop, smooth plastic placemat, or linoleum square
- Child-friendly acrylic paint
- Art paper
- Wet washcloths ready for a quick cleanup

1. Squeeze a small amount of paint onto the work surface, and encourage your child to spread the paint with his hands. You might like to use one color or explore color mixing by using two (or more).
2. Encourage your child to use his fingers to make marks in the wet paint surface. Older children will be able to make images using their fingers to make lines and shapes.
3. Place a sheet of paper onto the painted surface and smooth down. Then lift for the magical reveal!

Exploring Cardboard Combs

Experimenting with the different patterns made with a series of simple cardboard combs takes monoprinting to a whole new level, especially for young children who are not yet ready for making images of their own.

Gather your materials:

- Thick cardboard cut into pieces approximately 4 inches x 2 inches
- Box cutter (adult only)
- A smooth surface to work on—a glass tabletop, smooth plastic placemat, or linoleum square
- Child-friendly acrylic paint
- Paper

1. Adult only: Using the box cutter, cut one long edge of each cardboard rectangle into a regular pattern similar to the examples shown. The impression made will vary according to the thicknesses of both the comb teeth and the empty spaces between them.
2. Squeeze a small amount of paint onto the work surface, and allow your child to spread the paint with her hands.
3. Encourage your child to explore the impressions made in the paint by the different cardboard combs.
4. Place a sheet of paper onto the painted surface and smooth down. Then lift to reveal a print of the patterns made.

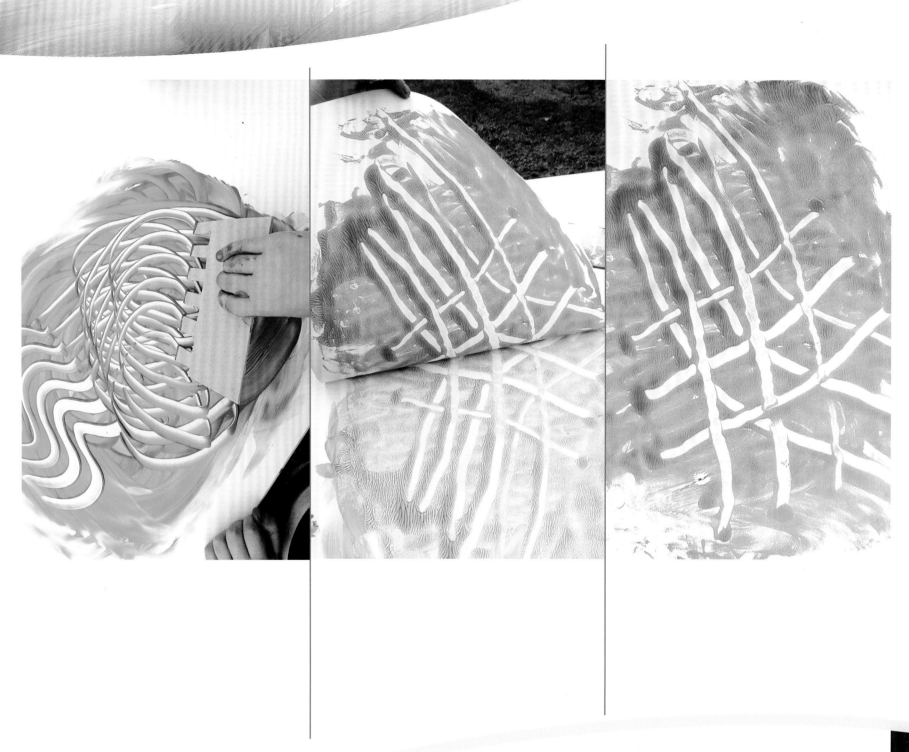

Pattern Printing with Found Objects

Experimenting with household objects to investigate the imprints they leave behind provides a wonderful introduction to pattern making. The range of objects available for use is only limited by your imagination, allowing for a range of interesting ongoing printmaking opportunities. Limit each pattern printing encounter to just one family of objects, as in the example below.

Gather your materials:

- Child-friendly acrylic paint
- Smooth Styrofoam meat tray (or similar)—one for each paint color
- Kitchen sponge—one for each paint color
- Paper printing surface
- Objects to print with—see suggestion list

1. Place one kitchen sponge onto each tray, and squeeze a reasonable amount of paint of one color onto each sponge.
2. Show your child how to press an object onto a wet sponge and then press onto paper to make a print.
3. Repeat with a range of objects, noticing how their imprints differ from object to object. Tip: Pattern printing on large sheets of paper is a simple but effective way to make wrapping paper with children.

Easy-to-Find Objects that Make Interesting Prints

- Kitchen: potato masher, fork, spoon, bottle cork, cup, cookie cutters
- Toys: wheeled vehicles, plastic figures, plastic or wooden blocks
- Nature: leaves, seedpods, flowers, small stones, shells
- Body parts: fingers, hands, arms, feet, legs
- Recyclables: cardboard tubes, plastic bottles, bubble wrap, plastic onion or potato bag, plastic lids, scrunched paper bags or catalog pages
- Theme: create a themed collection such as lots of objects of one shape
- Fruit and vegetables: To experiment with a range of fruits and vegetables, cut them into chunky pieces or thick slices suitable to be easily held. Carve shapes into the flat surface of potatoes (metal cookie cutters are useful for this) or leave plain.

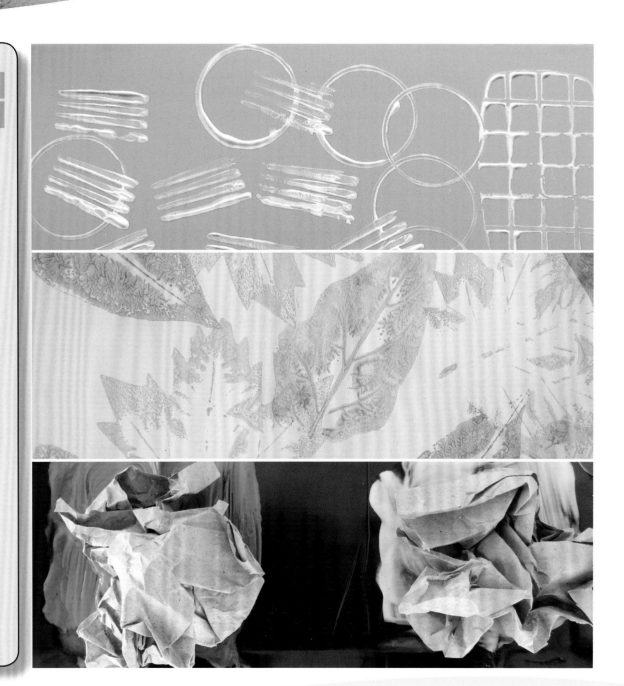

Four Ways with Crayon Rubbing

While crayon rubbing would not generally be associated with printmaking, the process creates interesting imprints that fascinate young children.

Outdoor Texture Hunt

Gather your materials:

- Paper (copy paper or similar works best)
- Crayons with paper wrapping removed

1. Place a sheet of paper over a tree trunk or brick, and show the child how to rub the side of the crayon over the paper to reveal an imprint of the texture underneath.
2. Send your child on a hunt to discover how many different textures she can find to make rubbings from around the yard. Young children may need help in understanding that a firm surface is necessary to create a successful rubbing.
3. When your child has created some interesting rubbings, consider cutting shapes from the completed rubbings to use to create a collage.

Indoor Rubbing Hunt

Gather your materials:

- Paper (copy paper or similar works best)
- Crayons with paper wrapping removed
- Flat objects suitable for rubbing, such as coins, puzzle pieces, keys, buttons, or ice-pop sticks

1. Show the child how to use the side of the crayon rubbed over the paper to reveal the imprint of a flat object placed underneath.
2. Send him on a hunt around the house to find other objects that he thinks will be suitable for making rubbings.
3. Encourage him to arrange his collection of objects underneath a sheet of paper and to use the side of the crayon to rub over the paper to reveal an imprint of the objects below. Older children may like to arrange their objects to create pictures, adding finer details with pencil or marker pen once the rubbing is complete.

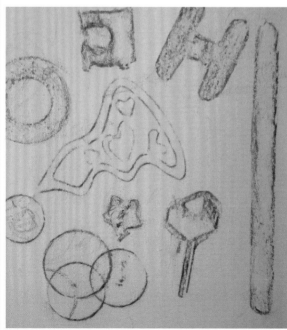

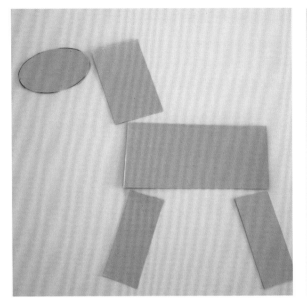

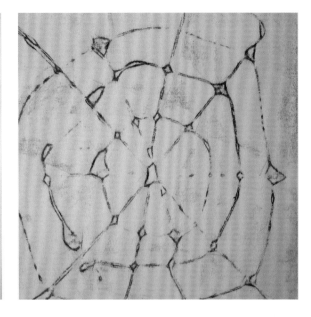

Rubbing Shape Pictures

Gather your materials:

■ Paper (copy paper or similar works best)

■ Crayons with paper wrapping removed

■ A range of shapes cut from card stock, corrugated cardboard, or sandpaper

1. Show the child how to use the side of the crayon rubbed over the paper to reveal the imprint of a cardboard or sandpaper shape placed underneath.

2. Encourage her to arrange the collection of shapes underneath a sheet of paper and to use the side of the crayon to rub over the paper to reveal the imprint. Older children can be challenged to arrange their objects to create pictures, adding finer details with pencil or marker pen once the rubbing is complete.

Rubbing Glue Pictures

Gather your materials:

■ Card stock for base

■ Child-friendly craft glue

■ Paper for rubbing (copy paper or similar works best)

■ Crayons with paper wrapping removed

1. Older children can make (or trace previously drawn) pictures with thick craft glue onto card stock.

2. Allow the glue to dry.

3. Encourage your child to use the texture of the glue on the card stock as an interesting base for crayon rubbing.

Woodblock Printing

Traditionally woodblock printing involves carving a relief image from a block of wood. However, for children it is much simpler to add to your block of wood than subtract from it, and there are a number of ways of doing so, which produce interesting textures and printed effects. For each of the following methods, start with a small block of wood that can be held comfortably by your child.

Ways to Make a Woodblock Stamp

1. Wool: Wrap lengths of wool or string around the block, and secure the ends with tape. Alternatively, use a hot glue gun (adult only) to attach pieces of wool arranged into a simple design to the face of your block. Once the glue is dried, the block will be ready to use for stamping.
2. Textures: Cut simple shapes from a range of textured materials, and glue each onto a block. Try bubble wrap, craft foam, corrugated cardboard, burlap, fake turf, and sandpaper for a range of textural imprints.
3. Glue: Create a range of simple motifs on a series of blocks. Allow the glue to dry.
4. To create a print, show the child how to dip the block into child-friendly acrylic paint. Test the print by pressing onto paper. If there is too much paint on the block, try spreading the paint onto a thin kitchen sponge first, as the sponge will absorb the excess paint.

Engraving

Wood and linoleum are very firm surfaces requiring sharp tools to carve, whereas Styrofoam or printing foam can provide a more suitable surface for small hands to engrave.

Gather your materials:

- Paper
- Foam painting roller or soft rubber hand roller
- Child-friendly acrylic paint
- Cookie tray
- Ballpoint pen
- Metal spoon
- Printing foam or Styrofoam surface to engrave Sheets of printing foam are available from educational art suppliers. Flat Styrofoam meat trays can also be engraved if the curved sides are removed.

1. Using light pressure, encourage the child to draw an image onto the foam using the pen.
2. Pour paint into the cookie tray and roll over the paint with the roller until the surface of the roller is evenly covered.
3. Roll the paint onto the foam surface until it is evenly covered.
4. Help the child place paper down onto the image surface and smooth with her hands or the back of a metal spoon.
5. Lift paper to reveal the printed image.

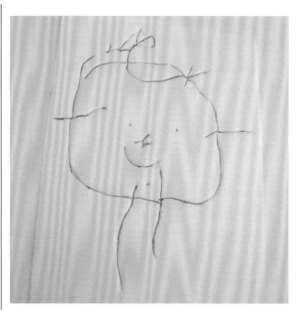

Seeing

Quality children's books feature the artwork of a range of professional artists. Use the pictures in a favorite book to weave a fictional story, or focus on an element of the art and explore it with your child.

- Talk about how the art is created; for example: drawing, painting, or printmaking
- Notice the art style featured; for example: abstract, impressionism, pop art, or realism
- Explore the details of the images
- Discover information provided about the life of the artist

Talking

Talk with your child about her printmaking throughout the creative process.

- Encourage your child to make predictions: "What sort of imprint do you think the bark will leave on the paper?"
- Acknowledge what your child is doing. "I see you are making swirling marks with your fingers in the paint," or "I see you are using the potato masher to make stripes on the page."
- Encourage your child to reflect on her art experiences. "How would you describe the imprint that the shell made?" or "Tell me about the image you have drawn onto your printing block."
- Describe what you see your child doing. "You are mixing the blue paint into red paint. What color are you mixing?"
- Encourage your child to describe the process used to create. "Tell me how you made your print."

Collage

Most days we head out of the house for a walk around our neighborhood. It is just one square suburban block, but walking with a 16-month-old can take quite a while. Her favorite part of our daily journey? Stopping to pick up a varied selection of seeds, nuts, flowers, leaves, and small rocks. We have a new collection every day.

I am amazed by what she spots on the path and the length of time our walk takes. She will find a little treasure, carry it for a few steps, and then gesture for me to carry it as she spots her next find. Today's completed collection—an autumn leaf, two small white stones, an interesting seed pod, a small nut, and two partly dried olives that had fallen from a tree laden with fruit.

Young children like to collect, sort, classify, organize, and create patterns—with toys, belongings, and little collections of everyday objects. It is, therefore, no surprise that children enjoy collage. After all, the process of composing and creating a collage combines all of these skills with another favored pastime–gluing!

Learning

Reasoning, logic, decision-making, and spatial awareness are probably not terms that we immediately associate with collage; however, children are practicing all sorts of language, mathematical, and scientific skills when they are thoughtfully engaged in creating collage.

The broad range of materials suitable for collage provides almost limitless potential for creativity. These materials are also perfect for matching, sorting, classifying, and arranging by a variety of attributes:

- Shape
- Size
- Color
- Texture
- Weight
- Substance

Providing a child repeated opportunities to create collaged artwork provides him with ongoing involvement in the physical process of learning within an enjoyable, creative context.

Doing

The simplest way to start out with little ones is by using a sheet of clear contact paper as the gluing surface. The child easily can arrange and rearrange flat objects onto the already sticky surface. Placing a second sheet of contact paper onto the first will secure the finished composition ready for display.

Once a toddler is ready for the challenge of using a brush, use flour-and-water paste as a suitable nontoxic alternative to commercial glue. Mix three tablespoons of all-purpose flour with enough water to make a thick paste. Show your child that the object being pasted needs to be placed directly onto the glue surface for it to stay in place. Children will likely need ongoing reminders of this principle for quite a number of gluing experiences. Paper and small pieces of fabric are best for gluing with flour-and-water paste.

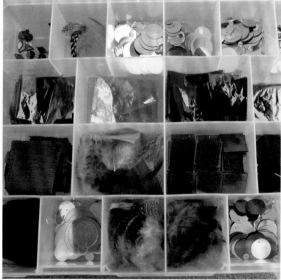

Choosing the Right Glue

When creating collaged artwork, match the right adhesive to the selected materials to ensure that everything sticks firmly and stays in place. As a general rule, the heavier the object being attached, the stronger the glue needs to be. The following list of adhesives will be sufficient for most early collage experiences:

■ Flour-and-water paste
■ Glue stick
■ Child-friendly white glue
■ Clear self-adhesive book covering

As with drawing and painting, collage can be used by older children as a means of communicating unique thoughts, ideas, and feelings. At around four or five years of age, a child can be encouraged to think more purposefully about both the materials he chooses, and the composition of those materials upon the work surface.

Materials for a particular artwork may be chosen according to color, shape, texture, or other obvious properties. Encourage your child to reflect upon which materials would best depict his intended purpose, including the ways in which these items might create a sense of emotion. For example, which colors, textures, or images would help to communicate joy? sadness? fear? Continuing to relate art to real-life interests and experiences will help to focus and motivate a child to create meaningfully and with a sense of purpose.

Adults can also encourage children to think about the elements of their composition by providing time for them to experiment with the arrangement of the materials before adding paste. Using art terms such as *line, color, shape, contrast,* and *composition* when talking with your child about his ideas can help him to develop a more descriptive art vocabulary.

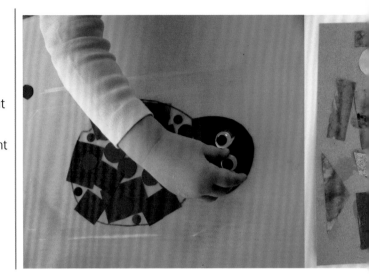

Common Art Terms

■ **Line:** a mark that forms part of the outline of a figure or shape
■ **Color:** the way the eye sees light as it is reflected off a surface; primary colors are red, yellow, and blue; secondary colors are orange, green, and purple
■ **Shape:** the form of an object or drawing
■ **Contrast:** the comparison of two different, often opposite, elements, such as light and dark
■ **Composition:** arrangement of elements in an artwork

One of the wonderful features of collage is how well it lends itself to the process of revisiting previous artwork. Drawings, paintings, and prints can be cut into pieces suitable for use in a collage, or collage materials can be pasted to prior creations.

Tear It Up!

Learning to rip and tear scrap paper is also a valuable fine motor skill for toddlers and preschoolers, so don't always reach for the scissors as a first choice when preparing for a paper-based collage.

Cut It Out!

Cutting with scissors is an important fine motor skill and is particularly relevant to the child's level of independence when working on collage and sculptural art projects. There is a lot of learning involved in using scissors, including holding the scissors correctly, using the fingers to open and close the blades, moving the hand forward as the paper is cut, and knowing how to support the paper with the other hand without inadvertently cutting any fingers! Young children need lots of regular opportunities to practice cutting with scissors.

Observe your child to determine her hand preference before scissors are introduced. Provide a pair of child-safe scissors designed for a right-handed or left-handed child.

Let your child practice using plastic scissors to cut playdough. This is a safe and playful way for young children to become familiar with holding the scissors and moving the hand and fingers to make the blades open and close.

Once the child is ready to cut paper, provide child-safe scissors with metal blades. Set clear boundaries for using scissors, such as only cutting paper and cutting only while sitting down. Remind the child that if she is not sure whether she is allowed to cut something, she should ask first. If the child has difficulty remembering which way to hold her hand when cutting, try sticking a little star just below the knuckle of your child's thumb. Remind her, "You need to be able to see the star for the scissors to work properly." Right

from the beginning, teach your child how to safely carry scissors when walking with them—with the handle up and blades down, fingers wrapped around the closed blades.

Offer lots of supervised opportunities to cut. Show the child how to hold the scissors correctly and how to open and close the blades by moving her fingers. Initially, just work on one snip at a time through a strip of paper that you hold taut. Once your child can hold the scissors and manipulate them relatively independently, provide lots of sheets of scrap paper for her to cut across. Recycled greeting cards, store catalogs, and pages from magazines are perfect for this purpose. Lightweight card stock and craft foam also work well, as the heavier weight helps to keep the cutting surface flat.

Cutting along a defined straight line is the next step in learning to control scissors, but children need lots of experience freely cutting before attempting this task. Cutting along a gently curved line will follow, and eventually, the child will master cutting around large, closed shapes. Provide the child with lots and lots of opportunity to practice at each stage. Don't push her beyond what she is capable of, and once the child loses interest, leave cutting for another time.

Seeing

A valuable part of collage-making is collecting materials, and it is easy and fun to involve children in this process. Before beginning a collage, talk about the theme or idea your child has in mind for his artwork. Ask which colors, textures, shapes, or images he thinks will convey his ideas, and use his responses to guide you in a treasure hunt for suitable materials.

Sources for Collage Materials

- In the garden
- Around the home
- At the park
- Out in the neighborhood
- In magazines
- Among hobby materials
- In the recycling box
- In the shed or garage

Ideas for Material Collections

- Textiles: wool, fabric, ribbon, lace, rickrack
- Craft materials: craft foam, buttons, string, small wooden shapes, doilies, feathers
- Decorative materials: sequins, beads, jewels, glitter
- Household items: small nuts, bolts, small tiles, matchsticks, ice-pop sticks, wallpaper, paint sample cards, sandpaper
- Recycled materials: plastic bottle tops, canceled postage stamps, catalogs, magazines, newspaper, small boxes
- Papers: scrapbooking, textured, colored, metallic, recycled, previously drawn or painted artwork, aluminum foil, cellophane

- Images: photographs, magazine pictures, previous drawings, greeting cards, postcards
- Natural items: seeds, nuts, leaves, sticks, dried flowers, grass, weeds, hay, small shells, small stones, sand

Does your child like to collect little treasures? Here are some ways to keep and display these collections within your home.

- **Sort It:** Using a sectioned box or tray or an egg carton, encourage your child to sort small collections.

- **Stick It:** Use contact paper to create a simple collage to display on a wall, bulletin board, or window.
- **Hang It:** Glue objects onto ribbon, and hang them from a small branch to create a mobile.
- **Photograph It:** Instead of keeping each collection, help your child to take photographs. Print and store the photos in an album of her very own.
- **Tape It:** Buy your child a spiral-bound sketchpad, and let her tape her collections in place to create a scrapbook of memories.

- **Keep It:** Together, decorate a small treasure box to keep collections in.
- **Display It:** Dedicate a shelf or a tray upon a shelf as a display space for your child's collections. To keep the size of the display manageable, teach your child the rule "one in/one out." For each item that she keeps, another finds a new home.

Talking

Well-known children's authors and illustrators Eric Carle, Jeannie Baker, and Lauren Child use collage to create their enchanting book illustrations. Carle's colorful animals, Child's beloved characters, and Baker's insightful, detailed treasure troves of texture can provide oodles of creative inspiration for the young artist.

As you look at these illustrations with your child, use questioning to help him notice the finer details:

- "What is the first thing you notice in this picture?"
- "What do you think the artist wanted us to focus on in this picture? What makes you think that?"
- "What message or emotion do you think the artist was trying to communicate through the piece?"
- "What more can we see here?"
- "What materials has the artist used in this collage?"
- "Is there a main, dominant color, pattern, or texture within the illustration?"
- "Has the artist used any interesting techniques that we might try ourselves?"

Sculpture

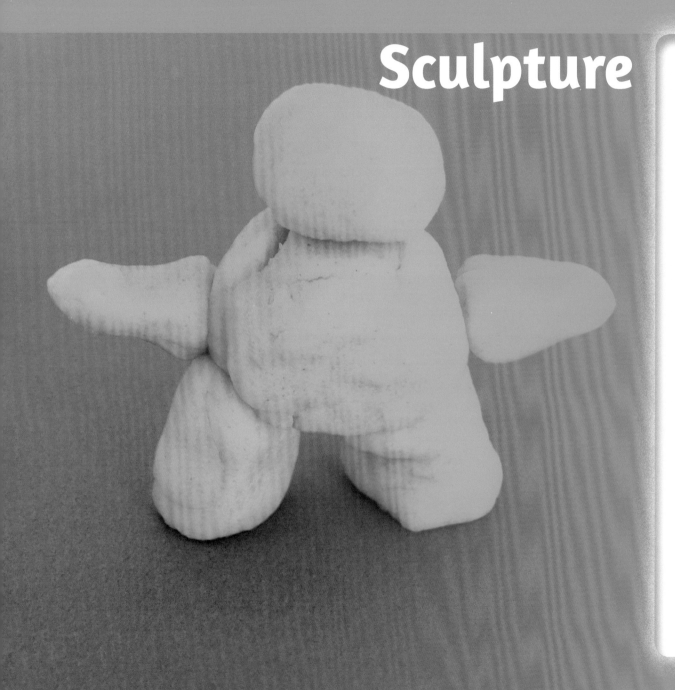

"The wheel keeps falling off. How can I make it stay on?"
"What can I use to make the ears?"
"Why doesn't the glue stick? It isn't working!"
"This is too big; it doesn't fit. Is there one that will go here?"

It is easy for an adult to tell a child why something doesn't work or to provide her with an easier solution to a problem. What is more difficult is to take a step back, to show restraint by not proffering the correct answer, and to instead support the child through the process of solving the problem independently.

The three-dimensional nature of sculpture adds a whole new level of learning to the creative art-making process. In the process of making creative choices and solving structural problems, children are developing behaviors and traits important to all learning—the importance of planning, patience, and perseverance, the process of trial and error.

Learning

Creating sculpture involves fashioning or shaping materials into three-dimensional form. From the first time a baby plays at stacking blocks, she begins to explore the challenges of arranging three-dimensional objects in a sculptural manner. Creating with dough, playdough, clay, boxes, and wood are just some of the ways young children continue the process of learning to sculpt. When working with each of these materials, the child faces a new set of construction challenges unique to the physical properties of the material and the processes required for manipulating it. With regular opportunity for repeated encounters with each material, mastery over these processes and concepts develops.

- Choosing materials that best suit her intended purpose
- Deciding the appropriate techniques for manipulating and joining materials
- Considering the scale and shape of individual materials
- Balancing the overall sculpture

Sculpting has the potential to focus learning and to bring a child's interest in a topic or theme to life. Imagine the joy of a child who is fascinated by dinosaurs creating her own large-scale replica from boxes and found materials, or the enthusiasm of a child who loves trains building a miniature world from papier-mâché, just as the model train collectors do. A child's interest can be a wonderful motivator, and a sculpture-based project with a level of challenge appropriate to the developmental capabilities of the child has the capacity to drive and reinforce learning in many ways, through all of the creative and problem-solving processes involved.

Doing

Sculpting mediums and their unique properties offer children diverse opportunities to learn ways of fashioning and joining. Some materials require carving or molding, others hammering and gluing or cutting, tying, and taping. Provide children with many opportunities to create with different types of sculpting material to expand the opportunities for learning physical-manipulation and problem-solving skills. The following project and material examples offer a diversity of processes and can be easily adapted for the age of your child.

Starting Out with Dough

Playdough is generally the first sculpting material provided to toddlers and is an excellent medium for helping children to develop control and strength in the muscles in their fingers and hands—important to learning to handle a writing implement. Extend the learning and creative opportunities of dough:

- Encourage your child to use his hands to flatten, shape, and join the dough, maximizing the opportunity for developing motor control skills and allowing for a greater level of creative response.
- Provide a bowl of natural materials for your child to use with the dough—small sticks, stones, shells, and seedpods work well.
- Provide a selection of marking tools—a plastic

knife, a pencil, an ice-pop stick, or a drinking straw—and observe your child's natural responses with these limited tools.

- Provide dough in a range of colors, or add glitter or glow-in-the-dark paint to enhance the experience.
- Change the texture of the dough by adding a little sand, uncooked rice, dried lavender, or rose petals, and encourage your child to explore the ways these differences alter the construction capabilities.
- Add cut pieces of drinking straw and matchsticks to extend the sculptural possibilities of a ball of dough.
- Provide a plastic knife and a pair of child-safe scissors as a way of practicing the use of these everyday tools.
- Provide a range of decorative elements— sequins, jewels, beads, buttons, pipe cleaners, and short lengths of ribbon and lace.

As an alternative to playdough, use salt dough, which can be baked to harden small objects. Your child can then decorate with marker pens, paint, or collage. (Some parts may need reattaching with glue following baking.)

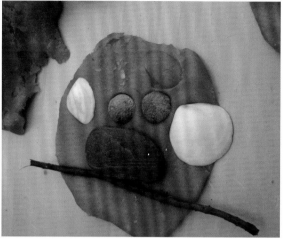

PLAYDOUGH

2 cups all-purpose flour
2 cups water
1 cup salt
4 tablespoons cream of tartar
2 tablespoons of vegetable oil
food coloring (optional)
Combine flour, water, salt, cream of tartar, oil, and a few drops of food coloring in a saucepan. Stir continuously over a medium heat until the dough comes together as a ball. Remove from saucepan and knead for five minutes. To make dough with more than one color, separate cooked dough into sections and create a shallow well in each. Add a few drops of color to each well, fold the dough over, and knead the color through.

SALT DOUGH

2 cups all-purpose flour
1 cup water
1 cup salt
food coloring (optional)
If you wish to color the dough, add a few drops of food coloring to the water before blending it into the flour and salt. Mix the ingredients thoroughly, and knead until smooth. Bake finished pieces at 200 degrees for two hours (thicker pieces may require more time). Let your child paint or add decorative details once the piece is cool.

Modeling Clay

Modeling clay is a natural next step from playdough, once young children have stopped mouthing objects. Available in packets of colorful sticks or as larger single-colored blocks, modeling clay generally requires more work to soften and model, which is great for strengthening hands and fingers.

Clay is a wonderful sculpting medium for children to work with. As with all art mediums, initially children will enjoy exploring the capabilities of this new and unique substance. Although as adults we may feel that it is very similar to dough, clay actually provides many different sensory associations and requires greater hand strength and dexterity to manipulate.

The mess factor of clay may be off-putting to adults, but white porcelain clay is much less messy than the red-brown terra-cotta variety, and thoughtful preparations can help to contain the mess.

- Organize the tools ahead of time, laying them out on the work surface.
- Work on a plastic placemat, linoleum, or a piece of waxed paper to not only provide a defined, easy-to-clean space for creating but also to ease moving the completed work.
- Teach children to clean up small pieces of dried clay with a ball of damp clay.
- Keep clay well covered with plastic or within its sealed container to reduce drying out.

Ways of Working with Clay

- Clay slabs: Use a piece of fishing line (adult only) to cut a flat slab of clay for your child to use. If necessary, smooth over with hands or a rolling pin.
- Imprinting: Explore the imprints left by a range of everyday objects from around the home or outdoors.
- Carving: Remove areas of the clay slab by scratching or carving the surface. Potential carving tools include a pen, pencil, ice-pop stick, matchstick, or plastic knife.
- Building: Use the clay slab as a stable base on which to build a clay sculpture.
- Pinching: You may remember learning to make clay pinch pots in elementary school. Make a pinch pot by starting with a small ball of clay. Encourage your child to press his thumb into the middle of the ball to make a well. Keeping his thumb in the well, help him pinch the clay between his thumb and forefinger to form the clay into the walls of a pinch pot, rotating the ball as he works.
- Coiling: Encourage your child to roll dough with her hands to make snakes, sausages, and spaghetti. Show her how to coil the clay snakes into pots, smoothing the coils to make smooth sides in the pots.

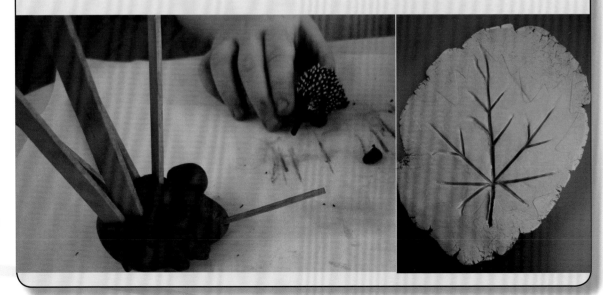

Clay Pictures

While modeling clay can be used with many of the same tools and accessories as playdough, it is also great for making colorful pictures.

Gather your materials:

- Modeling clay in a range of colors
- Thick cardboard base

Break off pieces of selected colors one at a time, and show your child how to warm them by cupping and kneading them with his hands. Let your child push the pieces onto the cardboard, forming selected shapes with fingers.

Clay Mosaic

A slab of clay is the perfect base for children to create a mosaic pattern or picture. Mosaic typically involves arranging and fitting together small pieces of colorful, hard materials. Experimenting with mosaic involves children in purposefully exploring color, shape, and texture in three-dimensional form.

Gather your materials:

- Clay
- Rolling pin
- Cookie tray
- Mosaic materials, such as eggshell, small plastic tiles, buttons, sequins, aquarium gravel, or beads
- Food coloring (optional)

1. To prepare the eggshell, clean shell halves thoroughly in warm, soapy water. Once dry, divide the shell into a series of small bowls—one for each color you would like to use. Add a few drops of food coloring, and mix until the shell is thoroughly coated, adding more color until the desired intensity is reached. Lay the shell out to dry on a sheet of waxed paper. Where necessary, gently break the shell into pieces, being careful not to make the pieces too small.

2. Encourage your child to roll out a flat slab of clay onto the cookie tray. Let her push the mosaic pieces into the surface of the clay using firm, even pressure. Continue until the surface is covered.

3. Set aside and allow the clay to dry. Should you wish to keep the completed mosaic, apply a layer of sealing medium, such as child-friendly Mod Podge, to help preserve this delicate work.

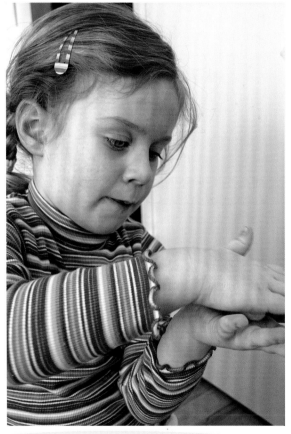

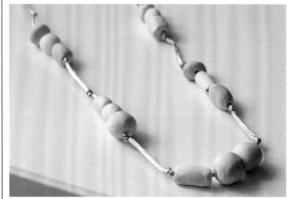

Clay Beads

Gather your materials:

- Air-dry clay
- Bamboo skewer
- Child-friendly watercolors or acrylics
- Small paintbrush
- Clear matte finishing spray (adult only)
- Thin ribbon or decorative string

1. To make the beads, roll small pieces of clay into selected bead shapes—spheres, cubes, cylinders, egg shapes.
2. Help your child use the bamboo skewer to gently pierce a hole through each bead.
3. Leave beads to dry according to the directions on the package of clay.
4. Encourage your child to decorate the beads by painting with watercolors or acrylic paints. Older children might like to add patterns or smaller details with a fine brush and metallic paint or a fine-line permanent marker.
5. Once the paint is dry, let your child thread the beads onto bamboo skewers.
6. Adult only: Holding a skewer with some beads on it, spray the beads lightly with the finishing spray, outdoors and away from your child. Prop the ends of the skewer across a bowl or small box, and leave to dry.
7. Let your child thread the dried beads onto a length of narrow ribbon or decorative string. Space the beads evenly and tie a simple knot between each bead (or group of beads) for an extra-special look.

Constructing and Joining

Making objects from clay can be tricky and involves planning, problem-solving, and perseverance. As your child explores sculpting clay figures, use the following joining processes to help your child learn how to hold a sculpture together.

- Smooth the joint between attached pieces to help them stay together.
- Make a 1:1 clay-to-water mixture called *slip,* which can be painted on with a brush or dabbed on with fingers to join two pieces together. First, scratch the surface with a plastic knife; then, apply a little slip and press the two pieces together.
- Use a toothpick, matchstick, or bamboo skewer as a support, for example, when joining an arm to a body.
- Remove small surface cracks by dabbing the clay with a small, damp sponge before smoothing with a finger.
- Should the clay begin drying prematurely, lightly spray hands with water before continuing to sculpt.

Construction with Boxes and Found Materials

What cannot be made from a cardboard box? Raid your recycling bin, and you will find a wealth of three-dimensional objects of all shapes and sizes suitable for constructing sculptures. Box construction allows children to work on a larger scale than most other sculpture experiences, and even the simplest project requires extensive problem-solving about the ways materials fit and join together. Tape and strong glue are imperative to success, but scissor skills can also be important.

Dedicate a large plastic tub as your child's box of useful materials, and fill it with the following collectables:

■ Cardboard boxes of various shapes and sizes
■ Paper towel tubes
■ Plastic tubs, such as butter and yogurt containers
■ Plastic cookie and candy trays
■ Plastic juice bottles
■ Plastic lids of various sizes
■ Pieces of cardboard of various weights
■ Bubble wrap
■ Egg cartons

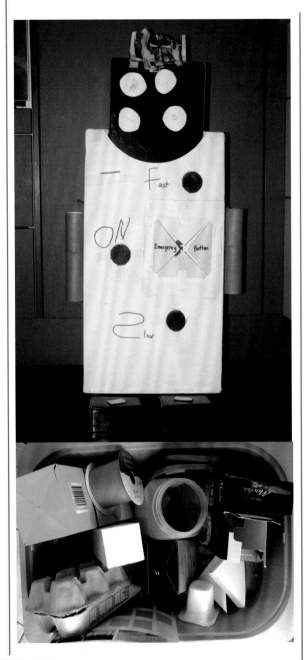

The following materials may also enhance the level of detail added to found-material projects:

■ Fabric, leather, and vinyl scraps
■ String
■ Elastic
■ Colored paper
■ Felt-tipped markers
■ Rubber bands
■ Ice-pop sticks
■ Matchsticks
■ Drinking straws

Vary the creative experience by sometimes allowing children freedom to choose what to make and other times focusing construction efforts on a current topic of interest.

Packing Peanuts

Packing peanuts (the kind made from vegetable starch) are a quick and easy sculpting material—no glue required! All you need is spot of water to stick them together, so a box of peanuts and a damp sponge can make for hours of three-dimensional fun and problem-solving. You can purchase them at office-supply stores, or just save them from shipping packages.

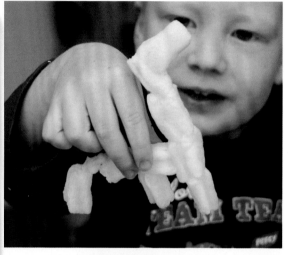

Ice-Pop Stick Snowflakes

We are told that no two snowflakes are exactly the same—what an exciting fact to share with children as they work at creating their very own ice-pop stick snowflakes.

Gather your materials:

- Ice-pop sticks
- Child-friendly white glue
- Waxed paper
- Watercolors or marker pens
- String or ribbon

1. Working on a waxed-paper base, let your child glue ice-pop sticks together to create a unique, snowflake-like formation.
2. Once dry, she can peel away the snowflake from the paper and decorate the snowflake with watercolors or marker pens.
3. Add string or ribbon and hang.

Woodwork

Woodwork allows children to use their own hands to build, and building seems like such a grownup task! Woodwork with real tools engages children with lots of problem-solving; is excellent for the development of eye-hand coordination and finger, hand, and arm motor skills; and can be a real test of perseverance.

Ask about wood offcuts at your local picture framer, lumber supply, or home project store. Soft woods (pine or balsa) and composite woods (medium-density fiberboard (MDF) or plywood) are generally lighter and easier for children to hammer nails into. Safety note: Always supervise your child closely when she is working with tools. Do not leave her unattended.

A Word about Arsenic in Scrap Wood

Before giving scrap wood to children, make sure it has not been treated with an arsenic-compound preservative. Although most building materials in the United States have not been treated with arsenic compounds since 2003, scrap wood milled before 2004 may contain arsenic. If you are not sure, do not give the wood scraps to your child.

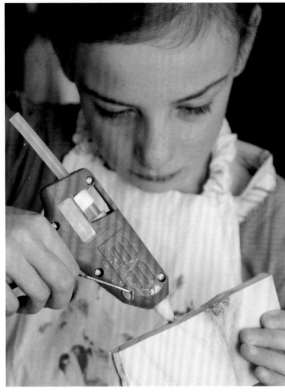

Woodworking Tips and Materials

- Sand any rough edges to reduce the chance of splinters.
- Present children with pieces in a range of sizes, shapes, and lengths.
- Wooden circles can be made with a circular drill bit.
- Include short lengths of dowel.
- Provide a variety of tools, such as a hammer (small, lightweight adult hammers are best), large-headed nails, wood glue, sandpaper, measuring tape, level, handsaw, ruler, and pencil.

Papier-Mâché

Papier-mâché has been used as an important creative technique in the fields of puppetry, costume making, and theatrical set design for many years. Fortunately, it also offers infinite uses for working with children on all manner of sculptural projects. When letting your child create using the typical paper-strip papier-mâché technique, think about the following factors: the glue, the base, and the application.

Virtually any liquid glue can be used for creating with papier-mâché, including flour-and-water paste, paper glue, wallpaper paste, or white craft glue. The chosen paste should be diluted with water until it is slightly runny. Adding 3–4 tablespoons of table salt to the glue can help to inhibit mold growth as the papier-mâché dries.

Common Base Materials

- Inflated balloons
- Shapes cut from thick box cardboard
- Rolls or balls of newspaper
- Recyclables including boxes, cartons, tubes, and plastic bottles
- Wire mesh
- Bowls or other vessels to act as a cast (covered with a grease base such as Vaseline to prevent the papier-mâché from sticking to the cast)
- Masking tape

Depending on the nature of the woodwork project, the following items might also be useful:

- String
- Fabric pieces
- Vinyl or leather pieces
- Ice-pop sticks or matchsticks
- Driftwood, shells, seedpods

- Rubber bands
- Wooden dolly pegs
- Small tiles
- Metal washers
- Plastic bottle tops (with premade holes)

Applying the Papier-Mâché

1. Let your child help you tear sheets of newspaper into strips that are approximately 1 inch wide.

2. Put the diluted glue into a large bowl or bucket. Show your child how to dip one strip of paper into the paste at a time, saturating it completely and smoothing off excess paste with his fingers.

3. Apply the strip to the papier-mâché base, smoothing it into position with your fingers. Repeat until the base is covered with two to three layers of overlapping paper strips.

4. Allow to dry completely.

5. Add further layers as needed, allowing the sculpture to dry every two to three layers until it reaches the desired shape and thickness. Finishing the sculpture with a layer of clean, white newsprint or paper towel will make painting or decorating the completed sculpture easier.

6. Once complete and thoroughly dried, the sculpture can be primed (as necessary) and painted with child-friendly acrylics.

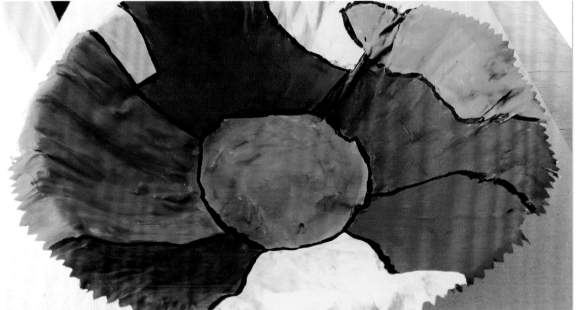

Papier-Mâché Pulp

Papier-mâché pulp adds a whole new level of flexibility to what you can create with paper and glue!

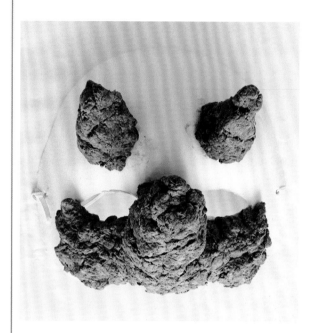

Gather your materials:

- Newsprint
- Plastic tub
- Hot water (adult only)
- Table salt
- Glue

1. Let your child help you tear newsprint into small pieces, no larger than 1 inch square.
2. Place the pieces into a large plastic tub and cover with hot water. Soak overnight.
3. Add 3–4 tablespoons of table salt to help slow mold growth as the pulp creations dry. Knead and squeeze the soupy newspaper-and-water mix by hand until the paper breaks down. If required, beating or blending the mixture will further refine the pulp.
4. Sieve and squeeze out excess water until the pulp is virtually dry.
5. Knead in a generous amount of glue until a clay-like consistency is achieved.
6. Mold the pulp into desired shapes, and apply to a selected sculpture base. Allow to dry thoroughly, reattaching any loose parts with strong glue as necessary before painting and decorating.

Seeing

Taking a series of photographs as your child works on a sculpture is a great way of allowing her to revisit her work. By looking at the pictures and talking about the processes she used, a child reinforces the learning that took place, especially as she discusses any challenges she faced and solutions she found. Watching your child's processes as she works and jotting down your observations will help to complete this picture of learning. Plus, it is much easier to store photographs and words than it is to store each three-dimensional sculpture that the child creates!

The wonderful thing about sculpture-based activities is their potential as an ongoing project over a number of art-making sessions. Paint makes a completed sculpture come alive, and drawing can add exquisite finer details to a collage, so try something new or combine two or more art-making techniques to find out what develops. Revisiting completed structures to add surface decorations with drawing, paint, or collage extends the creative potential of a project. There are so many options for adding detail to sculpture:

"First, we made the legs. If you make them too tall then the body will fall over."

"Roll the body into a ball shape. No, an oval shape."

"We used the matchsticks to make the arms and legs stick."

"Last, we made the head."

Buttons	Ice-pop sticks	Permanent markers	Sticks
Dried flowers	Lace	Ribbon	Stones
Fabric	Leaves	Seedpods	String
Felt-tipped pens	Matchsticks	Sequins	Wool
Glitter	Paint	Shells	

Talking

Successfully encouraging a child to solve construction difficulties when sculpting requires close observation and questioning to understand what the child is thinking, to focus his attention, and to scaffold his problem-solving attempts. When your child appears stuck in the creative or construction process, try the following methods of guiding him to find a solution:

■ Ask for clarification: "It looks to me like you are trying to attach the tube to the box. Would you like to tell me more about what you are doing?"

■ Verbalize the problem: "The arm keeps falling off that side of the body. What other things could you try to help it stay in place?"

■ Suggest an alternative material or technique: "Is there another type of tape in the drawer that might work?"

■ Remind him of previous successes: "Remember the time you made a papier-mâché turtle? What did you do then to hold the head in place while the glue dried?"

■ Consider peer support: "Do you think that there is anyone else here who might be able to help with this problem?"

Creative Challenges

In its purest form, process art is about children freely exploring an art medium. Children must have regular blocks of time for open-ended, child-led exploration, especially when introduced to new art mediums. Exploration provides children with the opportunity to understand the capabilities of a material and to respond to it individually, both in terms of how they use it (within reasonable limits) and what they choose to create with it.

There will, however, come a time where most children seek more direction from an adult, asking, "What should I make?" or stating, "I don't know what to do with it." Arriving at this stage will be different for every child. Alternatively, there may be times when you wish to use an art medium as a means for exploring and sharing his knowledge, ideas, or feelings relating to a specific topic. Setting a creative challenge can be an excellent way of extending both the creative response and learning opportunity of an art-making project. The most effective creative challenges are those that are based on what fascinates the individual child.

Children develop interests in all manner of things, from more common childhood obsessions such as dinosaurs and superheroes to the more unique and unusual, such as garbage trucks or a specific brand of shoe. Popular culture or recent events, such as a field trip or a vacation, also may stimulate interests. Listen to a child's conversations and closely observe him at play to determine his current interests.

 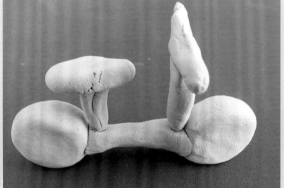 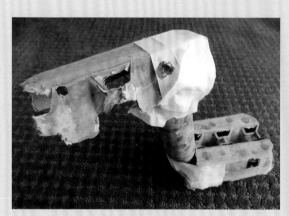

Setting a Creative Challenge

Partner an idea or question related to a child's interests with an appropriate creative medium that the child can use to formulate her unique response. When planning a creative challenge, ask yourself the following questions:

- Is this challenge fun and interesting to the child involved?
- Is it open-ended, allowing for the unique response of the individual?
- Is it based on an idea or question the child has about the interest we have been exploring?
- Is it appropriate to the age and developmental capabilities of the child involved?
- Are the materials suitable for the child to use to represent and communicate what she knows or is learning?

Creative Challenge Examples

- Draw a superhero with his very own superhero costume representing his super powers.
- Use the clay to make a bicycle that stands up by itself.
- We read that the color of many insects acts to camouflage them from their predators. Take the watercolor painting you made of an insect last time, and use these collage materials to create an environment that provides a safe place for your insect to hide.
- Use the modeling clay to create a model representing the most interesting thing that you learned or saw at the aquarium today.

Textiles

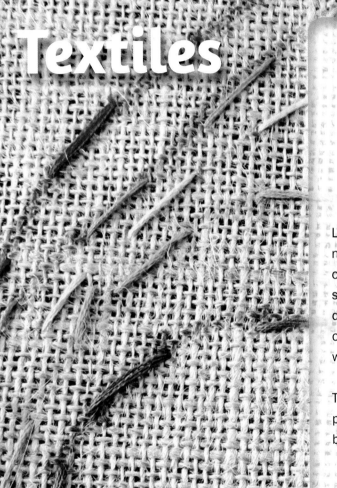

*Did your child have a special soft toy
or piece of cloth that
provided him comfort as a baby?
Texture is important not only to our senses
but also to our emotions. When something feels good,
it can comfort and relax us; harsh textures can feel
abrasive and cause excessive discomfort.*

Linen. Brocade. Silk. Velvet. Cotton. Burlap. Satin. Taffeta. Tulle. Corduroy. The sheer number of different types and textures of fabric and fibers available provides a veritable feast of textural stimulation for children, inviting them to explore and learn through these tactile sensations. Textiles provide children with the opportunity to learn to discern between and describe textures such as soft or rough, warm or cool, woolly or silky, smooth or bumpy, furry or prickly and to develop preferences based on their own physical and emotional responses to what they feel.

Textiles can provide an interesting base for familiar creative techniques such as drawing, painting, and collage, but also lend themselves to new ways of creating using sewing, beading, and weaving.

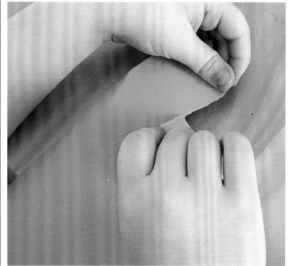

Learning

In the process of learning to walk, a baby needs time and opportunity to master the many small steps—learning to roll, sit, crawl, stand, and cruise the furniture—that are so essential to her reaching that all-important final goal. In the same way, a child needs encouragement and opportunity to master the many skills necessary in to learning to write. This group of skills includes arm steadiness, arm and hand control, and hand and finger strength and dexterity. Also essential is the development of eye-hand coordination, increasing levels of self-control (including patience and perseverance), and the ability to concentrate closely on what she is doing. When you consider the amount of control required to hold a pencil and to direct it to efficiently form letters, it is easy to see why activities for young children that strengthen and train the muscles in the arm, hand, and fingers are so important.

Learning to write will generally be a much easier process for children who have had lots of opportunities for fun and playful practice to develop these skills. Regular and varied opportunities to create art are perfect for this purpose. Art-making experiences develop fine motor skills through opportunities for scribbling, drawing, painting, blending, stamping, sculpting, taping, printing, cutting, tearing, gluing, molding, engraving, carving, pressing, rubbing, rolling, squeezing, weaving, hammering, stitching, and more. When choosing appropriate art-making activities for your child, consider his current level of fine-muscle control, his ability to concentrate, and his level of emotional control, especially in how he deals with frustration. Younger, inexperienced, and less-confident children may require a greater level of adult encouragement and support and shorter periods of time engaged in art-making.

Be aware of the individual child's development and follow his lead during the process of creating, to support his feelings of accomplishment and enjoyment of art. Feeling good about making art leads to a willingness to engage in further creative experiences, and each experience the child engages in takes him one step closer to the later goal of learning to write.

Doing

Dropper Painting

Combine pipettes and thin, bright colors to create a unique fabric.

Gather your materials:
- Eyedroppers or pipettes
- Food coloring or liquid watercolors
- Small paint cups
- Spray bottle of water
- Cotton fabric, paper towels, or white coffee filters
- Newspaper

1. Dilute the food coloring or liquid watercolors as desired, placing one color in each paint cup.
2. Place fabric or other painting surface onto a bed of newspaper to absorb excess color.
3. Lightly spray the painting surface with water.
4. Show your child how to use the eyedropper or pipette to transfer the liquid color from the paint cup onto the painting surface. As she creates, talk together about how the colors spread across the surface and combine.
5. Leave the fabric to dry thoroughly.

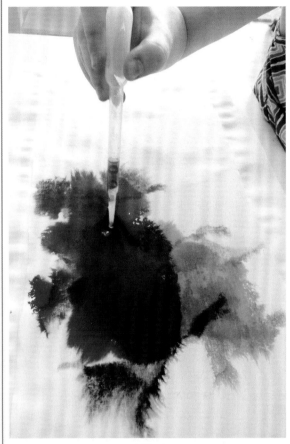

Drawing and Painting on Fabric

Fabric provides a great alternative surface for experimenting further with familiar art mediums, such as marker pens and paint.

Gather your materials:

- White cotton fabric
- Thick box cardboard
- Masking tape
- Paint (see note below)
- Permanent felt-tipped markers
- Iron (adult only)

Painting on Fabric

Should the artwork be intended to form part of an item that will be regularly laundered (for example, a piece of clothing), then commercially produced fabric markers and paint may be best. Alternatively, nonwashable acrylic paints and regular permanent marker pens will remain permanent if ironed with a hot iron before washing, but they may fade more readily. For items that will not need to be laundered, regular child-friendly acrylics will work just as well.

1. Tape the cotton fabric to the cardboard with masking tape to hold it steady as the child works.
2. Let the child draw his image directly onto the fabric with the markers.
3. If using acrylic paints, dilute 1:1 with water. Add painted details directly to the fabric.
4. Allow fabric to thoroughly dry.
5. Once dry, iron with a hot iron (adult only).

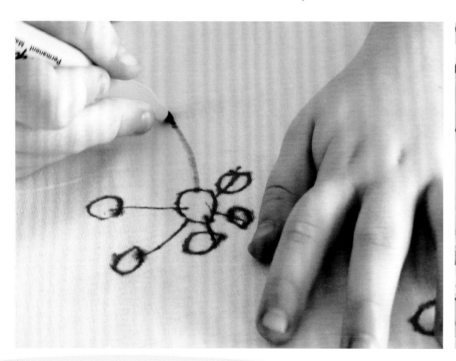

White Glue Batik

Create a unique design on fabric with this twist on the batik process—the use of white glue makes it a much more child-friendly alternative to the traditional hot wax.

Gather your materials:

- Child-friendly white craft glue in a squeezable bottle
- Acrylic paint (do not use washable paints for this activity)
- Water
- White cotton fabric
- Cardboard
- Masking tape
- Plastic tub or bucket
- Iron (adult only)

1. Tape fabric to the cardboard with masking tape to hold it steady as the child works.
2. Let the child create his design directly onto the fabric by squeezing the glue from the bottle. Older children may wish to lightly sketch their designs first with a pencil.
3. Put aside until the glue has completely dried.
4. Dilute acrylic paint colors by combining with a little water. The more water you add, the less intense the chosen colors.
5. Encourage the child to completely cover the fabric with paint, and allow to thoroughly dry.
6. To remove the glue, soak the fabric in a tub of warm water for 20 minutes, refreshing the water after the first 10 minutes so that it stays warm. As necessary, gently rub away the glue from the fabric with your finger.
7. Once the glue is completely removed, hang the fabric to dry and then iron with a hot iron (adult only).

Fabric and Fiber Collage

Fabric, fibers, and sewing accessories add texture and interest to collage artwork.

Gather your materials:

- Fabric (offer a variety of scraps, strips, larger pieces or shapes of fabric; a range of textures, designs, colors)
- Fibers (yarn, ribbon, rickrack, embroidery thread, elastic)
- Sewing accessories (buttons, beads, sequins, zippers)
- Strong, child-friendly glue
- Box cardboard, canvas board, stretched canvas or other firm surface to create upon
- Child-safe scissors

Offer a wide variety of materials, and encourage your child to create and explore. Talk with him as he works, asking questions about his thoughts and ideas.

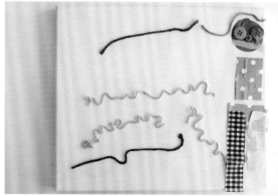

Printing onto Fabric

Create personalized fabric designs by printing on fabric with familiar household items.

Gather your materials:

- White cotton fabric
- Thick box cardboard
- Masking tape
- Paint
- Styrofoam trays (or similar)
- Collection of objects, such as plastic lids, cookie cutters, comb, and so on

1. Tape the fabric to the cardboard with masking tape to hold it steady as the child works.
2. Squeeze a small amount of paint onto each tray.
3. Press objects into paint and then onto fabric to print.
4. Set fabric aside to dry.

Weaving with Textiles

Weaving develops both fine motor and thinking skills and is a useful way to introduce a range of textiles to young children.

Gather your materials:

- Thick cardboard
- Ruler and pencil
- Scissors
- Tape
- Textiles such as yarn, embroidery thread, string, ribbon, rickrack, and fabric strips

To make the loom:

1. Cut the piece of thick cardboard to the preferred size.
2. Mark regular intervals along both the top and the bottom of the cardboard, being sure that the marks line up top and bottom. Smaller children will need widely spaced threads on their looms, but the threads can be placed closer together for older children.
3. Make a small slit at each mark using scissors.
4. Tape the end of a piece of yarn at the top left corner on the back of the cardboard, close to the first slit.
5. Run the yarn through this first slit so that it now sits at the front of the loom.
6. Bring the yarn down to and through the corresponding slit on the bottom edge of the cardboard.

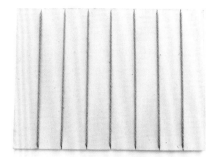

7. Bring the yarn forward through the second bottom slit, and then bring the yarn to the top second slit and push it through to the back.
8. Continue in this manner, working up and down, until you reach the final slit. Finish with the yarn at the back of the loom and attach with tape to hold firm.

To weave:

1. Starting at the bottom of the loom, show the child how to thread her chosen textile strip over and under the strings of the loom, pulling the strip through as she goes.
2. If using long pieces of textiles, once she has reached the far side of the loom, show the child how to come back, but this time going under where she previously went over and vice versa.
3. Show the child how to start with her second weaving strip by now going under where she previously went over the strings of the loom.

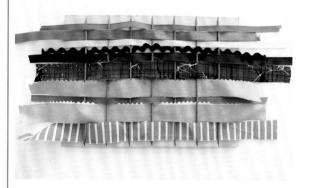

4. If the child accidentally pulls her strips too far through, try taping the end of the strip to the back of the loom before she begins.

While many textile-based activities, such as weaving and sewing, are often considered craft activities, the same techniques and materials can certainly be used to create works of art. Art is created when the child learns control of exactly what to create and how to create it with the available materials. In this way, he has space to share his own knowledge, ideas, or feelings through an individualized response. Success relies primarily upon the supportive adult thinking carefully about the presentation of the materials, the level of direction as to how they are to be applied, and the nature of the support given as the child works.

Of course, as with the process of introducing any new art-making media, demonstrating simple techniques for using a material successfully helps the child to produce more satisfying results and reduces any frustration that he cannot accomplish the vision that he has for the materials. The following suggestions for sewing with children are presented in an approximate order of difficulty, to assist you in selecting which activities will best suit your child.

Beginning Sewing

Depending upon the level of fine motor control, young children can be introduced to simple hand sewing from around the age of two and a half; although, success at this age will depend largely upon interest and motivation.

Gather your materials:
- Plastic canvas or nonslip, plastic drawer liner
- Embroidery hoop
- Plastic needle
- Yarn or thick embroidery thread

1. Stretch the plastic canvas tautly in the embroidery hoop.
2. Cut a section of yarn in a length that your child can manage easily.
3. Tie the yarn to the needle so that the needle does not slip off.

4. Knot the other end of the yarn, thread it through the canvas or drawer liner, and allow the child to stitch in a free-form fashion, encouraging him to pull the needle and thread all the way through (until the yarn is taut) each time.

Adding Embellishments
As your child is able, introduce decorations for your child to explore in his sewing.

Gather your materials:
- Large, blunt-nosed metal needle
- Embroidery thread
- Decorative embellishments with good-sized holes, such as large, chunky buttons; large beads; oversized sequins; small bolts or washers; and small, unused keys

1. Let your child continue working with the plastic canvas or drawer liner, but invite further interest by adding suitable decorative embellishments. Offer a variety, and consider making your own decorative notions by cutting out colored cardboard or felt shapes and adding holes with a hole punch or scissors.
2. Show your child how to fit the needle and thread through the holes of the embellishments. As appropriate, introduce the idea of pushing the needle back down through

to the back of the fabric close to where the decorative element was added.
3. Encourage your child to add the embellishments on the front of the fabric, but allow for creativity.

Sewing with Fabric
The relatively loose, open weave of burlap makes it a good first actual fabric for children to sew on.

Gather your materials:
- Piece of burlap
- Embroidery hoop
- Blunt-nosed needle
- Embroidery thread
- Decorative embellishments
- Fabric or permanent marker

1. Stretch the burlap onto an embroidery hoop to help to hold the fabric steady as the child works.
2. Repeat the experiences of free-form stitching and adding decorative embellishments on the burlap.

3. Invite the child to draw an image to embellish the burlap using a fabric or permanent marker. As children learn to aim the needle with more control (at approximately five years), they can be taught to form small stitches to outline their images.

4. As your child becomes comfortable with sewing, introduce felt as an alternative fabric to use for each of the processes outlined above.

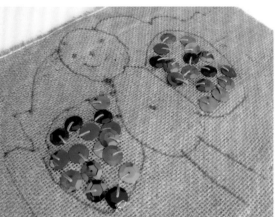

A Note about Needles

Plastic needles are often available for purchase through educational-resource stores. When choosing metal needles, look for large needles that are easier for small fingers to hold, with a large eye to hold yarn and embroidery thread, and with blunt, rounded tips. Tapestry needles, bodkins, or ballpoint needles are a good first choice.

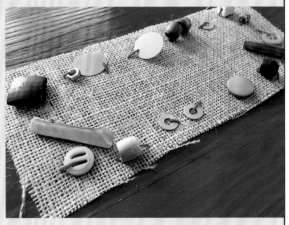

Seeing

Whether it be setting out a large, fresh piece of paper alongside watercolors all ready to use or presenting a collection of interesting items on a brightly colored tray to weave together, taking a moment while your child is otherwise occupied to set the stage for creating—preparing an invitation to create—is a great way to capture her interest.

This key is not dictating how the child explores or what she is to create; rather, it is simply presenting materials in an aesthetically pleasing manner all ready to use. And it really does take just a minute.

There are a number of simple things you can do to enhance your invitation to create:

- Clear the table of all unnecessary items.
- Lay a large piece of colored paper or a colored plastic tablecloth on the table.
- Group creative materials according to type, color, size, or texture.
- Present materials in small baskets, glass jars, or on a decorative tray.
- Place inspiring objects on the table, such as a vase of bright flowers, a mirror, or items related to a current interest.
- Add a small lazy Susan–style rotating tray to display project-specific art materials (especially handy for the center of the table when more than one child will be using the space to create).

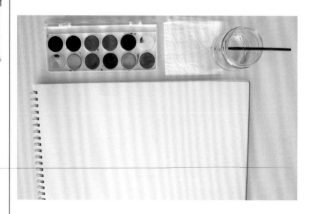

Talking

Asking good questions encourages children to think beyond the obvious, and in the process they practice using higher-order thinking skills such as problem solving, brainstorming, creating, thinking critically, analyzing, and evaluating. Consider the learning and conversation potential each of the following pairs of questions:

"Can you see the clouds in the sky?" versus "I wonder, how do the clouds get into the sky?"

"What is this part of the elephant called?" versus "What would you do if you had a trunk?"

"Can you see the lizard?" versus "Why do you think lizards lie in the sun?"

"What type of dinosaur is this?" versus "Do dinosaurs have friends?"

"Can you see the bird flying by?" versus "What would happen if you could fly?"

"What is that noise?" versus "What would that noise look like if we tried to draw it?"

"Which of the balls floats?" versus "How does the ball stay on top of the water?"

"Can you find the red wool?" versus "How many different ways could you use this wool?"

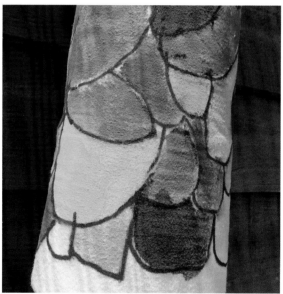

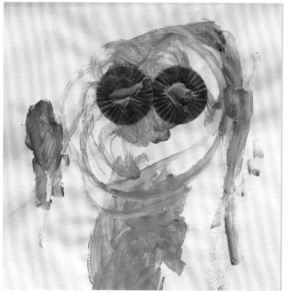

Digital Photography

Digital technology has changed the way we see and record our world, making the act of taking a photograph simpler, more accessible to greater numbers of people, and less expensive as a creative pastime. Children who experience this technology often exhibit what appears to be a natural understanding and control of digital media devices from a very young age, which is unsurprising given that it is the nature of young children to seek to understand their environment and the various elements within it.

Placing a digital camera into the hands of a child is a wonderful way to capture a child's-eye view of her world. Once the initial novelty of using the camera wears off, a child will often turn to capturing objects, people, and events of importance to her. A camera can also be a useful visual tool to help a child to focus on specific elements of her physical world—colors, shapes, lines, patterns, textures, light, and dark—all relevant to creativity, but also concepts important to other areas of learning, such as math and science.

Learning

When it comes to choosing a digital camera for a young child to use, first consider his age and stage of development, your knowledge of the child, and his likely interest, engagement, and propensity for proper handling. Adults are often nervous about handing over their own expensive digital cameras or mobile phones with camera technology, but there are a number of options available.

Digital cameras specifically made for young children are drop proof but typically feature very small viewing screens and are not ideal for use indoors or in conditions of low light. Alternatively, letting a child use an older, secondhand digital camera or a cheap or disposable model will enable him to take better quality photographs in a range of light conditions, with less concern for the potential of a broken camera.

Teaching a Young Child to Use a Digital Camera

Demonstrate how to use the camera properly, then let the child explore the device.

- Show her how to wear the camera strap around her wrist.
- Demonstrate holding the camera securely so as not to drop it.
- Remind her to keep fingers away from the camera lens.
- Turn the camera off after each use to preserve the battery life.
- Show her how to look through the viewfinder or at the digital display to line up the subject of the photograph.
- Tell her the importance of being still and not moving the camera while taking the photo.
- Show and tell preschoolers or older children what each part of the camera is called and what it does.

As a child gains confidence with using the camera, demonstrate the following:

- The difference that moving close to the object or subject can make to a photograph
- How an object can be photographed from different angles (front, side, down low, or up high) to achieve different results
- What happens when photographs are taken in low-light settings, with and without a flash
- The value of taking more than one shot of an object or subject, but set a limit as to the maximum number of photographs she may take of the one item

Doing

Head Out on a Photo Hunt

Similar to a treasure hunt, a photo hunt requires the child (or group of children) to find and photograph a range of objects or subjects meeting specified criteria. Photo hunts can easily be adapted to represent a range of themes.

- A color or collection of colors
- A shape or collection of shapes
- A number or the numbers 1–10
- The letters of the alphabet
- Visual patterns
- A range of textures
- Up and down

- Fast and slow
- Elements of nature
- Parts of the body
- Emotions
- Ways of moving
- Shadows

This activity is easily adaptable for children of different ages. Provide clues verbally one at a time for older toddlers or younger preschoolers, or draw a list using picture symbols for older preschoolers and other pre-readers.

Host a Photography Exhibition

One meaningful way to show that you value a child's photography is to offer to help her to host an exhibition of her work. Before preparing an exhibition of her own, research the availability of age-appropriate photography exhibitions featured at galleries in your local area, and consider taking a field trip together to look at the work on display. This can be an effective way to engage and motivate children to create their own galleries and provides a point of reference for understanding the features of an exhibition.

Once your child is ready to prepare for her exhibition, decide the following:

- Discuss a possible theme for the photographs (she may not wish to have a theme at all).
- Plan how she will present her photos. Will they be mounted onto a base or framed in some way?
- Choose and print the photographs to be included in the exhibition.
- Brainstorm a relevant title for each image, and print title cards.
- Make a list of people she would like to invite to view her exhibition, and prepare the invitations.

PERSON
2011

Creating Photo Books

*The crocodile jumped out of the water
when the man threw in the bucket.
It gave me a big surprise because
I couldn't see it in the water!
—Four-year-old recalling a visit
to a reptile park*

Providing a child with a camera to record a field trip or vacation is a great way to preserve his memories of the event. Plus, once the trip or holiday is over, you have a wonderful basis for creatively recording his recollections of these adventures.

Decide your preferred method of presenting the completed story, as this will affect the process of creating the book. You can present the photos and text in a number of different ways:

■ In a commercially produced photo album with standard photo-sized pockets into which you can slide photos and text-filled cards

■ By sticking the photographs and writing the text directly onto sheets of lightweight card to be stapled, punched, or bound together

■ As a commercially printed photo book available through a printing service, many of which can be ordered online

1. Look through the collection of photographs with the child, discussing which he would like to include in his book.

2. Print selected photos or upload them to the commercial photo-book software, if using a book-printing service.

3. Ask the child to tell you about each photograph, and transcribe his words to accompany each image. The text may be typed or handwritten—whichever is easiest and works best for your chosen presentation.

4. Collate the photographs and text into his photo book.

5. Enjoy revisiting these adventures together.

Photo Storybook Ideas

You don't have to go on a trip to encourage children to create their own photo storybooks. The following list of themes is intended to encourage a child to create a record of specific elements of her own history:

■ A Day in the Life of . . .
■ In the Morning
■ The Story of Me
■ About My Family
■ Around My Home
■ Out My Window
■ In My Garden
■ I Love to . . .
■ My Favorite . . .
■ Did You Know?
■ True or False?
■ Learning to . . .
■ The Adventures of . . .

We saw a sun bear. He was perching in his home.

Seeing

Taking time to look through and talk with a child about his photographs helps the child to focus on the individual elements of the image captured. Support a very young child with simple, positive comments:

"I like the way you have photographed the tiger as he is walking by."

With older children, ask questions to focus attention to more specific details, such as:

"Which photograph captures your eye the most? Which makes you really want to look closely at it?"

"Which photograph has best captured the subject? Why do you think it looks so good?"

"Which photograph do you like the most? Why?"

"Which photograph didn't work quite how you intended? Why do you think that happened?" (for example, movement of the camera or low lighting)

Talking

Sometimes adults forget that literacy is not just about reading and writing. Literacy includes all of the ways people create and use language. Learning to confidently and competently speak is an essential component of early literacy learning. Photographs can be a powerful visual tool for stimulating oral communication, encouraging a child to do the following:

- Remember past events
- Organize her thoughts to share her recollections
- Talk about places, events, people, feelings, and emotions
- Practice the correct use of new vocabulary specific to an event or experience
- Reinforce facts and lessons learned through an experience
- Talk about her emotional responses to an experience; for example, joy on a family holiday
- Talk about what she likes or dislikes about a particular image

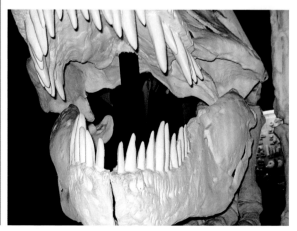

Natural Materials

*Puffs of white, fluffy clouds moving
across a blue sky,
The ever-changing shape of the moon,
The silvery path of a snail traversing a
garden path,
The sound of rain thundering on a tin
roof,
The tall, straight trunks of trees along a
hiking trail,
Early morning dewdrops glistening on a
spider's web,
The potential splash of a muddy puddle.*

The natural world is full of color, light, texture, shape, line, sound, and movement, all of which are captivating to the young child.

Encourage children to take an interest in and learn more about the wider world, inspiring them to create through outdoor explorations and include elements of nature in their art projects. Helping children to find the beauty in nature; to see outdoor spaces as places of fun, inspiration and recreation; and to learn about the interconnectedness of all elements of the environment can act to spark a child's nurturing spirit. After all, our children are the future caretakers of the natural world.

Learning

When recently driving past an area of newly cleared land, my three-and-a-half-year-old remarked, "There's no bush now and nowhere for the kangaroos to live!" We live in an area previously surrounded by large areas of natural bush land that is being cleared to make way for new housing projects. It's true—clearing the land is destroying the natural habitats of many native species of flora and fauna.

It seems logical that a child encouraged to spend time exploring outdoors is more likely to develop an interest in respecting and caring for the environment. Children who spend ongoing, regular time outdoors have the opportunity to closely observe changes in the natural environment. They are in the best position to learn about weather, the seasons, natural resources, plants, insects, birds, and other animals. Although it may require a little more organization, children who live in predominantly urban environments can also enjoy regular opportunities to learn about the natural world through visiting parks, nature reserves, or other green spaces within the community—anywhere there is sand, water, grass, or trees, there is sure to be something new to discover.

Appreciating Natural Environments

When exploring outdoors with children, be sure to model and talk with them about respecting all elements of the natural environment. Familiarize yourself with the rules of protected nature reserves, and guide your children as they explore.

- Recognize harmful insects, and learn what to do when they come across one
- Be gentle with creatures they examine (when it is appropriate to touch)
- Leave everything as they found it—if they move it, put it back
- Take their trash with them when they leave, or dispose of it properly
- Leave bark, leaves, flowers, and seedpods on the plants and trees. If they wish to collect some, only take those that have fallen to the ground.

Doing

Creating Temporary Nature Art

Introducing children to the work of British sculptor Andy Goldsworthy—best known for his sculptures created from natural materials including rocks, leaves, sticks, snow, and ice—is a wonderful way to engage their curiosity with the idea of creating with natural materials. You can find photos of his work online by typing "Andy Goldsworthy" into your search engine.

For the majority of his natural art, Goldsworthy collects his materials from the place where he is working and uses little more than his bare hands and imagination to create stunningly beautiful temporary works. Photographs of his work are available in a series of books by the artist and provide a wonderful resource for talking with children about the choice and use of materials, shape, color, size, patterns, and problem-solving.

Start by getting outdoors to see what materials are available to collect, then invite your child to create her own temporary art installations from natural materials.

Rocks	Feathers	Pinecones	Driftwood
Leaves	Flowers	Seedpods	Sand
Sticks	Grasses	Seashells	Soil
Branches	Mud	Sea glass	Snow

Encourage children to look at the shapes, colors, and sizes of the materials they collect to create their own nature-based works of art. While it is most likely that completed artwork of this nature will be temporary, it is easy to extend the creative experience by encouraging each child to photograph her completed works.

Making Mud Pies—Is It Art?

Some would argue that the concentration and dedication of young mud-pie makers in creating and finishing their pie creations is indeed reflective of more permanent art-making endeavors. Whether it is or not, it certainly is a pastime to encourage, as it requires children to be outdoors. Regular outdoor play is crucial to all areas of development—physical, language, cognitive, social, emotional, and creative!

Collage with Natural Materials

Grab a bag or basket, and head outdoors to see what treasures you can discover that are suitable for creating a collage. Whether their art-making responses are a part of a creative challenge or are completely open-ended, children will enjoy collecting, sorting, naming, and manipulating their collected materials as part of the collage-making process.

Gather your materials:

■ A collection of natural materials

■ Strong, child-friendly glue

■ A firm surface to create on—box cardboard, canvas board, stretched canvas, wood

■ Scissors (optional)

1. Gather a variety of natural materials with your child.

2. Sort through what he has found.

3. Encourage him to create a collage with his treasures.

Leaf Collage

Sometimes limiting a child's art-making to just one type of material can be a good thing. Due to their range of shapes, sizes, and colors, leaves have the potential for stimulating lots of discussion and learning. Looking at the range of colors of foliage (even from one type of tree and especially as the seasons change) naturally lends itself to talking together about tone: Can we sort these leaves in order from lightest to darkest?

Rock Drawing

Story stones are a wonderful tool for encouraging oral storytelling with children aged three years and up. Your child can create a personalized set of story stones by drawing her own set of images or simple motifs.

Gather your materials:

- A collection of clean, smooth, flat stones
- Permanent markers or paint pens in contrasting colors

1. With your child, make up a story or repeat a favorite story.
2. Talk with your child about the images she can draw to tell the story.
3. Have your child draw the selected images with markers or paint pens on the stones. Allow the ink or paint to dry thoroughly before using.
4. Use the stones to tell and retell the story.

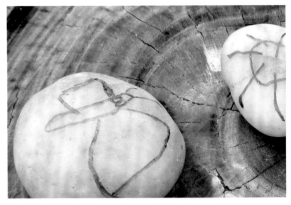

Drawing on Hot Rocks

A challenge for older children, hot rocks provide an interesting canvas for wax crayon designs.

Gather your materials:

- A collection of clean, smooth, flat stones
- Cookie tray
- Newspaper
- Wax crayons with paper wrapping removed
- Oven mitts

1. Place rocks onto cookie tray and heat inside a 300 degree oven for 15 minutes (adult only).
2. Carefully remove the rocks and place onto a bed of newspaper.
3. Reminding your child that the rocks are hot, allow him to decorate the surface of the rocks with the crayons. Encourage him to wear oven mitts to protect his hands, and carefully supervise him while he works. As he draws, the crayon will melt onto the rock. When the rock cools, the crayon will also cool and will reharden.

Nature Weaving Two Ways

Why not set this brainstorming question to children before heading outdoors on a weaving hunt: What do you think we can find outdoors that is long, thin, pliable, and just right for weaving?

Leaves	Hay
Bark	Pine needles
Sticks	Vines
Grass	Stalks of herbs

Weaving on a Cardboard Loom

Follow the instructions found on page 97 to make a loom from cardboard and wool or string.

Gather your materials:

- Natural materials found on your weaving hunt
- Cardboard loom
- Yarn or string

1. Make a cardboard loom.
2. Using the materials from her weaving hunt, encourage your child to create a woven masterpiece.

Decorating Sticks

Transform a sturdy stick by using it as the canvas for creating a multimedia work of art. It could even become a personalized talking stick for your family.

Gather your materials:

- A sturdy stick
- Child-friendly acrylic paint
- Hot glue gun (adult only)
- Decorative items, such as wool, string, ribbon, feathers, sequins, buttons, glitter, and small bells

1. Let your child paint the stick in any way she chooses.
2. Encourage her to add her choice of decorative items by tying them on or letting you attach them with the hot glue gun.

Weaving on a Branch

You will need a strong, forked branch for this activity.

Gather your materials:

- Strong, forked branch
- Wool, string, or ribbon
- Natural weaving materials

1. Starting at one side of the bottom of the fork, tie your wool to the branch.
2. Weave from side to side in a figure-eight formation. Looping the wool around each side of the fork at both the top and the bottom of the figure eight will provide additional support to the wrap.
3. Tie off the wool once you reach the top of the fork.
4. Encourage your child to add all sorts of wonderful natural materials that he found on his weaving hunt.

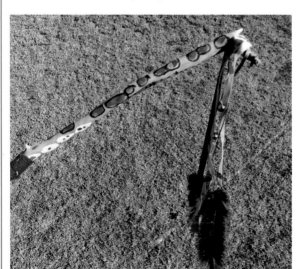

Ten Outdoor Spaces to Enjoy with Children

Visiting a range of outdoor spaces provides children with the opportunity to expand their knowledge of the natural world.

Beach	Campgrounds	Orchards
Creek	Nature reserves	Your own backyard
Botanical gardens	Riverbanks	
National parks	Farms or farmers markets	

Using Clay with Natural Materials

Given its earthy foundations, clay is the perfect companion for creating sculptural forms with natural materials. Found objects such as sticks, leaves, stones, and seedpods can be used to add details to (nonfired) clay sculptures. Natural materials are also fabulous for creating impressions by pressing into slabs of clay.

Textured Clay Relief Sculptures

Gather your materials:

- Clay
- Rolling pin
- Selection of natural materials

1. Cut a flat slab of clay and place it on a stable, flat working surface. Lightly smooth it with a rolling pin if necessary.
2. Encourage your child to make impressions by firmly pressing natural materials into the surface of the clay slab and then removing them. Explore the different impressions made by different parts of each object as well.
3. Working with families of objects, such as all different seashells or types of seedpods, provides for interesting discussions about the similarities and differences that you can see.

4. If your child wishes to make a plaque to be hung, use a pencil (or something similar) to add two holes to thread ribbon or twine through once the clay has dried.

5. Set the clay aside on a flat surface to dry thoroughly.

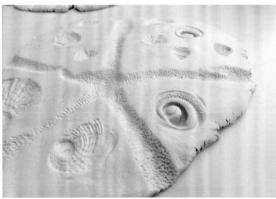

Creating without Paper

"We could draw the clues on the bark to get to the tree house."

Much of the skill of being creative is feeling both free and secure in the knowledge of oneself to produce and express original ideas and solutions. Introducing children to surfaces other than paper or canvas for creating on encourages them to look beyond the obvious when it comes to using familiar objects (in this case, natural materials such as bark or leaves) in new ways.

Bark
Thin wood slices cut from thick branches
Leaves
Branches
Stumps
Flat rocks
Seashells

But That's Not a Paintbrush!

Did you know that many artists paint not only with brushes but also with knives? A painting knife has a steel blade and is used by artists as an alternative tool for applying paint to canvas. Experimenting with different tools for applying paint is another way to extend a child's understanding of the capabilities of paint as a creative medium.

Many everyday items from around the home and garden can act as interesting paintbrush substitutes, each making their own unique impressions upon the painting surface. Here's a list of suggestions to get you started:

Large ice-pop sticks

Cotton swabs

Spoons

Bottle corks

Shaving brushes

Plastic knives

Sticks

Feathers

Sprigs of rosemary or other herbs

Seeing

Spending time outdoors encourages children to "see" with all the senses—sight, sound, smell, touch, and taste—all of which provide valuable sensory input to the developing brain of the young child. Make the most of outdoor time:

- **Look Closer:** Help young children to focus more closely on the smaller details with a magnifying glass, bug catcher (though be sure to return insects to their rightful home once done), or digital camera.
- **Listen Carefully:** Draw your child's attention to the sounds particular to the place you are exploring. Whether it is birds calling, leaves rustling in the wind, or waves lapping on the shore, helping a child to attend to what he can hear develops more effective listening skills.
- **Talk Together:** Take time to talk together about your discoveries and encourage children to share with others also. Retelling and teaching others are wonderful means of reinforcing one's own learning.
- **Use Your Imagination:** Lie back and look for pictures in the clouds. Make up a story together about the ants you see scurrying on the ground. Amble like bears or fly like birds. Look for opportunities to enhance the allure of natural spaces by adding a touch of magic to your adventures.

Talking

We were recently outdoors gardening when my almost-four-year-old discovered
that her plastic wading pool was partially filled with rainwater.
I was working close by when she called to me, excitedly telling me
how the pebbles she was throwing into the water were all sinking.
I asked her if she could find anything in the yard that might float instead of sink.
And the hunt was on!

Being outdoors with children and working together with natural materials provide invaluable opportunities to respond to teachable moments. Teachable moments are generally unplanned, child-initiated opportunities for learning. The fact that the child instigates the learning means that she is already switched on and motivated to make further discoveries. Recognizing teachable moments requires both careful observation and listening on the part of the adult, as well as responsiveness to what the child says and does. Maximize the learning potential of these opportunities:

- Ask good questions to encourage the child to explain her observations and theories: "Why do you think the ball and the bowl both float, but not the rock?"
- Follow the child's lead and do not be concerned if she loses interest. It is likely that she will revisit this learning again at some stage. Don't push.
- Keep the experience interesting, active, and hands-on, especially for younger children.
- Encourage preschoolers and older children to use art materials to record their experiences, observations, and theories.

Taking Art Further

"But my child has been obsessed with fairies/elephants/pirates forever!"

One of the wonderful things about art is the number of unique opportunities it offers to children to represent their knowledge of an interest, to share a passion, or to share an idea. When art is used as part of the process of learning, children have the opportunity to discover and explore, to express and to answer by using art-making materials to represent what they know, think, or feel.

For now, your child may have one strong interest or passion, but by providing time, space, a range of materials, and a number of creative challenges, you will continue to inspire her to learn not only about her interest, but to learn how to learn as well!

Mixed Media: Combining Techniques

Within the world of visual art, a mixed-media artwork is one that employs more than one art medium. Encouraging children to revisit previous artwork is a great way to generate interest in creating mixed-media pieces. There are possibly hundreds of ways to combine the art processes found throughout this book, but here are some simple suggestions to get you and your children thinking about the possibilities that mixed media offers to young artists:

- Cutting or tearing painted papers into shapes and using for collage
- Adding finer details to a painting or collage with marker pen after the paint or glue has dried
- Painting a canvas background and then pasting on characters or other images cut from previous drawings
- Adding additional color to crayon rubbings or drawings by painting over them with liquid watercolors
- Adding a third dimension to paper-based artwork (drawn, painted, or printed) by adding details with 3D collage materials

Art Out and About

Incorporating art into outdoor play or recreation time can open a whole new world of creative possibilities.

Being outdoors will often spark new ideas for using familiar art materials; plus, nature provides a whole new realm of inspiration for finding subjects to draw, paint, or otherwise create. Be ready to create outdoors whenever the sun is shining by keeping a basket or bin stocked with a bound sketch pad, a collection of drawing mediums, a glue stick, and a small tape dispenser. Extend the opportunities for creating by mixing up what else you include in your basket or box:

- A block watercolor palette; paintbrush; and a small, sealed jar of water
- A small, sealed jar of clay or playdough
- A pencil case with scissors, colored paper squares, ice-pop sticks, matchsticks, feathers, and other small items
- Pencil rolls are also great for taking along colored pencils, mechanical crayons, or felt-tipped markers

Being ready to make art whenever you are on the move can be as simple as keeping a pencil or marker pen and an unlined notebook in your handbag or car.

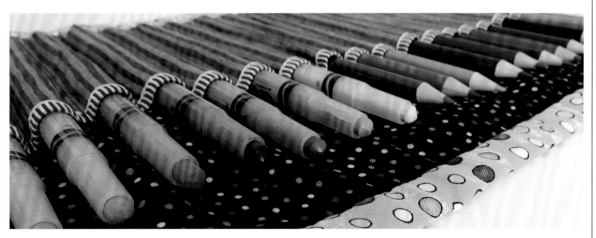

Appendix

The following lists are suggestions only—think of them as a wish list for stocking your art-supply cupboard! Project-specific materials are mentioned for each activity throughout the book.

General Equipment

Adult scissors

Camera

Child-safe scissors

Cups or jars for holding paint, glue, or water

Kitchen sponges

Painting easel—self-standing or tabletop

Pencil sharpener

Ruler

Styrofoam trays (or something similar)

Minimizing the Mess

Bucket

Newspaper

Painting smock or apron

Plastic or canvas drop cloth

Plastic tablecloth

Washcloths

Wet wipes

Drawing Materials

Candles (use paint wash to reveal images)

Chalk

Chalk pastels

Charcoal or charcoal pencil

Colored pencils

Crayons

Felt-tipped markers

Oil pastels

Pencils

Pens

Watercolor pencils or crayons

Whiteboard markers or crayons

Drawing Surfaces

Black art paper

Boxes

Canvas boards

Card stock

Chalkboard

Colored copy or art paper

Concrete surface

Graph paper

Leaves

Newspaper

Patterned scrapbook paper

Previous drawings or paintings

Sandpaper

Textured paper

Tracing paper

White copy or art paper

Whiteboard

Window or shower door

Painting Materials

Block watercolors

Child-friendly acrylic paint

Corks

Cotton swabs

Craft feathers

Fabric paint

Food coloring

Ice-pop sticks

Leaves

Liquid watercolors

Paint brushes—variety of sizes

Paint dotters

Plastic knives

Shaving brushes

Spoons

Sticks

Straws

Watercolor pencils

Painting Surfaces

Bark

Black art paper

Brown paper bag

Canvas

Card stock

Child-friendly acrylic paint

Colored copy or art paper

Cork

Crayons

Fabric

Household objects

Irregularly shaped paper

Large sheets of paper

Large, flat stones

Newspaper

Previously drawn or painted artwork

Printing foam or Styrofoam surface to engrave

Recycled items such as cardboard or egg cartons

Tiny pieces of paper

Wallpaper

White copy or art paper

Window or glass shower door

Wood

Printmaking Materials

Card stock

Child-friendly acrylics

Crayons

Household objects

Printing foam or Styrofoam

Small blocks of wood

Thick cardboard

Wool or string

Printmaking Equipment

Ballpoint pen

Cookie tray or similar

Foam painting roller or soft rubber hand roller

Metal spoon

Smooth plastic placemat or linoleum square

White craft glue

Collage Materials

Craft materials: craft foam, buttons, string, small wooden shapes, doilies, feathers

Decorative items: sequins, beads, jewels, glitter

Household items: small nuts, bolts, small tiles, matchsticks, ice-pop sticks, wallpaper, paint sample cards, sandpaper

Images: photographs, magazine pictures, previous drawings, greeting cards, postcards

Natural materials: seeds, nuts, leaves, sticks, dried flowers, grass, weeds, hay, small shells, small stones, sand

Papers: scrapbooking, textured, colored, metallic, recycled, previously drawn or painted artwork, aluminum foil, cellophane

Recycled items: plastic bottle tops, canceled postage stamps, catalogs, magazines, newspaper, small boxes

Textiles: wool, fabric, ribbon, lace, rickrack

Adhesives

Child-friendly paper glue

Child-friendly white craft glue

Clear contact paper

Flour-and-water paste

Glue stick

Hot glue gun (adult only)

Collage Surfaces

Aluminum foil

Canvas boards

Cardboard cut from recycled boxes

Card stock—match weight of card to materials being used

Paper

Stretched canvas

Wood

Sculpture Materials

Bubble wrap

Cardboard boxes of various shapes and sizes

Cardboard tubes

Clay

Dowels

Egg cartons

Modeling clay

Newspaper

Packing peanuts

Plastic containers, such as butter and yogurt
    containers

Plastic cookie and candy trays

Plastic juice bottles

Plastic lids of various sizes

Playdough

Salt dough

Scraps of cardboard of various weights

Wood scraps

Sculpture Accessories

Colored paper

Dried pasta

Drinking straws

Elastic

Fabric, leather, and vinyl scraps

Felt-tipped pens

Ice-pop sticks

Matchsticks

Metal washers

Paint

Permanent markers

Pipe cleaners

Plastic knife

Rubber bands

Seedpods

Shells

Small sticks

Small tiles

Stones

String

Wooden dolly pegs

Yarn

Adhesives

Child-friendly craft glue

Colored electrical tape

Masking tape

Packing tape

Painter's tape

Wood glue

Sculpture Equipment

Bamboo skewers

Baking paper

Cookie tray

Fishing line (adult only)

Hammer

Handsaw

Large-headed nails

Level

Measuring tape

Plastic placemat or linoleum scraps

Rolling pin

Sandpaper

Textiles Materials and Surfaces

Acrylic paint

Child-friendly craft glue

Fabric markers

Fabric paint

Fabrics: 100-percent cotton, burlap, felt

Fibers: yarn, ribbon, rickrack, embroidery thread,
    lace, elastic

Food coloring or liquid watercolors

Nonslip drawer liner

Other fabrics or fabric scraps chosen to represent
    a range of textures

Permanent felt-tipped markers

Plastic canvas

Sewing notions: buttons, beads, sequins, zippers

Small bolts and washers

Textiles Equipment

Embroidery hoop

Eye dropper or pipette

Iron (adult only)

Plastic needles

Round-nosed, metal needles

Spray bottle

Natural Materials

Bark

Branches

Driftwood

Flowers

Grasses

Hay

Leaves

Pinecones

Pine needles

Rocks

Sand, soil, mud

Sea glass

Seashells

Seedpods

Snow

Stalks of fresh herbs

Sticks

Surfaces

Bark

Box cardboard

Branches

Canvas boards

Flat rocks

Leaves

Stumps

Seashells

Stretched canvas

Thin slices of wood cut from thick branches

Index